R. Brannon
(8,16.16)
(928, 849, 1284)

god on your own

OTHER BOOKS BY JOSEPH DISPENZA

On Silence

The Way of the Traveler

The Magical Realism of Alyce Frank

Live Better Longer

The Serigraphs of Doug West

Will Shuster: A Santa Fe Legend

The House of Alarcon (novel)

Advertising the American Woman

Freeze Frame: A History of the American Film

Reruns: Cinema on Television

Forgotten Patriot

god on your own

FINDING A SPIRITUAL PATH
OUTSIDE RELIGION

Joseph Dispenza

Foreword by Thomas Moore

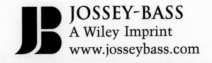

JOSSEY-BASS
A Wiley Imprint
www.josseybass.com

989 Market Street, San Francisco, CA 94103–1741   www.josseybass.com

Jossey-Bass books and products are available through most bookstores.
To contact Jossey-Bass directly call our Customer Care Department within the U.S.
at 800-956-7739, outside the U.S. at 317-572-3986, or fax 317-572-4002.

Jossey-Bass also publishes its books in a variety of electronic formats.
Some content that appears in print may not be available in electronic books.

Library of Congress Cataloging-in-Publication Data

Dispenza, Joseph, date.
God on your own: finding a spiritual path outside religion / Joseph Dispenza; foreword
by Thomas Moore.
p. cm.
Includes bibliographical references and index.
ISBN-13: 978-0-7879-8312-3 (cloth)
ISBN-10: 0-7879-8312-8 (cloth)
1. Spirituality. 2. Spiritual life. I. Title.
BL624.D586 2006
204'.4—dc22
2006004547

Printed in the United States of America
FIRST EDITION
HB Printing   10 9 8 7 6 5 4 3 2 1

CONTENTS

Teachers open the door.
You enter by yourself.

— CHINESE PROVERB

This book is dedicated to all my teachers.

FOREWORD

RECENTLY, I WAS interviewed by a regional magazine. I mentioned that I sometimes use Tarot cards when making a big decision. I got a letter back from a man who quoted the Bible against divination and said I was dead wrong and leading young people astray. I responded by asking him to lighten up his theology. I suggested that the Bible warns against a certain kind of magic that is indeed wrongheaded, but that I use the Tarot to jump-start my intuition. Hoping to find a little middle ground, I was disappointed to get another letter from him, even more condemning.

I have the sense that this man represents millions of people, in various religions, who grew up deep in anxiety that manifests itself in harsh, punitive, and joyless judgment of others. This is not religion in any vital sense of the word, but a profound twisting of what could be a source of life-affirming spirituality into some deathly, inhumane caricature. People who persist in this kind of religion suffer their highly constricted lives and paradoxically stand in the way of the world enjoying the meaning and self-affirmation that deep religion offers.

Joseph Dispenza and I have much in common. We know monastic life firsthand, and we know Christian theology.

When we were very young, something stirred to turn us toward an unknown spiritual focus; though the forms have shifted over the years, the path of seeking is intact. I admire many elements in his story, especially his willingness to pursue intuition in service of his unique spiritual destiny. He takes the spiritual life seriously and yet wears it lightly.

I know that this book can help many people who find themselves stuck between their old religious practices gone stale and the uncertain possibilities in front of them. Joseph's principles are solid. I am especially pleased to see his emphasis on avoiding spiritual seeking as a way to bypass the emotional issues that keep us stuck. If we go forward in our spiritual search and fail to deal head-on with the major problematical raw material of our past, and with emotions and fantasies that block the life in us, then our spirituality doesn't have much chance to be vital and honest.

We are all neurotic, some more than others. This means we all have a pile of raw material to sift through and refine. If you had an abusive childhood, you have a big pile to deal with. If you have had a drinking problem, your pile is thick and rich. The more difficult the stuff of your past, the more promising your future spirituality. As this book demonstrates so beautifully, spiritual seeking is not a pleasant safari through a lush landscape but a lifelong trek through jungle and desert. There will be moments of clarity and delight, but the way is challenging. It demands that you take your life seriously and, in the words of my namesake, Thomas More of England, not pin it on someone else's shirtsleeve.

On the other hand, Joseph makes it clear that certain gifted people may well appear at crucial moments and help you make important turns and leaps. But you have to be alert and willing to be their student. The lone spiritual path is not for those who think themselves superior to religions and churches. In fact, it is a humbler way.

I admit I was a bit shocked to read some of Joseph's words against religion. Especially in my doctoral studies in world religions, I developed a love of this word *religion,* and I still try to give it fresh life. To me, religion is a prerequisite for being alive as a human being. It is not just an outward and outmoded institutionalization of spirituality. It is a posture in life: reverence for life's mysteries, practice of contemplation and deep consideration of those mysteries, and consequent profound ethical sensitivity. Joseph speaks quite properly when he says that spirituality requires a life of service.

But I do think this difference is largely a matter of words— my concern for keeping religion alive. Joseph even tells us how to keep traditional teachings and practices fresh and meaningful. Nothing could be more important in this age of secularism, which is to say soullessness. Unfortunately, religious institutions often collude in keeping modern life secular by failing to understand sufficiently the prophetic and penetrating nature of the religious point of view.

I too live a monk's life, disguised as an ordinary citizen trying to get along. Contemplation, detachment, deepened sexuality, obedience to the spirit when it moves, community, reverence, and certain stillness can be part of an ordinary life. Spirituality is sensual, practical, and quotidian, if it is anything real at all.

Maybe Joseph and I can convince others to try the monastic life in the world and create an invisible monasticism. In the medieval world, monasticism was the source of learning, art, and moral sensibility. There is no reason a new, invisible monasticism cannot similarly revive culture and transform our current unconsciousness, materialism, and aggressiveness into intelligence, sensuousness, and mutual regard.

Thomas Moore

INTRODUCTION:
TAKING BACK YOUR SOUL

We find God in our own being, which is the mirror of God.
—THOMAS MERTON, *SEEDS OF CONTEMPLATION*

ONE NIGHT IN 1984, in a remote village in northern New Mexico, I stood barefoot before a path of hot coals about three feet wide and thirty feet long, trying to decide if I was going to walk on it, or walk away. I was told that at that moment the glowing red nuggets, half a foot deep, had reached the temperature automobile factories use to melt down scrap metal.

I hesitated there, my pant legs rolled up to my knees, my eyes fixed straight ahead at the fire-path, reminding myself to breathe. The hypnotic sounds of drumming filled my ears. I knew I did not have to do this, but on another level I absolutely knew I had to do it if I were going to break through to a new place inside myself.

I filled my lungs with the chill night air, let it out slowly, and made the first step onto the fire bed. Staring ahead, avoiding looking down at my feet, I took one step, then another, then another. The fiery coals felt like soft cinders under my feet. I made my way down the path with unhurried, deliberate steps, and at last reached the end. I stepped off the fire and onto the cool earth.

For a moment, I just stood there dazed and slightly numb. I had not been incinerated. The soles of my feet had not been scorched, had not turned to ash, had not even blistered. I had confronted one my greatest fears and moved through it. My body had survived fire.

Then, as if in slow motion, I lifted my eyes to a sky ablaze with starlight and sensed a rush through my body so powerful that for some time I seemed to be weightless and outside myself. In that thrilling moment I felt myself one with all of creation—one with the earth I was standing on, with the sky, with the stars, with all people, animals, trees, mountains, rivers, the very air I was inhaling. I felt truly alive, grateful for my life and my connection to all other living things.

For me, walking on fire led to a high spiritual experience, a sacred encounter with the Source of all life. That feeling stayed in me with varying intensity for several days afterward. In time, my life went on as usual, but somehow with more spiritual awareness and attention. The memory of the firewalk and its aftermath has remained with me all these years as a reference point—one of many that were to follow—for a spiritual life I have forged for myself outside of organized religion.

Long before I walked on hot coals that night in search of spiritual connection, I turned my back on the life of a monk and gave up my faith—the religion of my parents. I decided to seek the divinity, if there was a divinity, away from the traditions, rituals, and rules of Roman Catholicism.

I was born into a family of practicing Catholics and so grew up as a member in good standing of that religion. After graduating from Catholic high school, I entered an order of teaching monks and lived as a professional religious man for eight years. In monastic life, I had the opportunity to study the theology of my religion in great depth. My inquiries led me, in time, to question many of the beliefs I accepted blindly as a child and a teenager. The questions became spiritual issues for me, and finally and ironically they became blocks to my spiritual growth.

Leaving the faith of my childhood was not easy, particularly at that time, forty years ago, when attitudes about religion were considerably less flexible than they are today. Predicable pressures exerted themselves: the puzzlement and then the disapproval of family and friends, the embarrassment, the shame. Leaving religious life was even more difficult. When I gave up my religious vows, I received a letter from the Vatican that began, "Insofar as we are able, we release you. . . ." I had made my vows to God, you see, and therefore I was answerable to God for my actions. A disapproving family was one thing; a disapproving God was quite another—divine displeasure could endanger my immortal soul.

Years later, now, I see that walking away from religion has turned out to be a blessing. It led me to many fascinating areas of soul exploration, from past-life regression and dream work to faith healing and shamanism, and just about everything in between. It allowed me to investigate the splendid spiritual traditions of other cultures and go deeply into a mystic realm in search of my spiritual Source. Leaving the confines of organized religion opened me to the possibility of creating my own spiritual life, one that gives direction and meaning to all I do and all I am.

In my search, the challenge for me has been to try to recognize spiritual truth when I see it and discard the rest—particularly the superficial offerings of popular metaphysical thought and practice. My background was in the rigorous discipline of traditional theology; I wanted my spirituality to be solid. Looking back at the process I went through on my journey from organized religion to personal spirituality, the most discouraging times were when I realized I had no roadmap to guide me even a little. I left the spiritual "certainties" of religion because I was finding no nourishment there, but outside religion there were no certainties of any kind, only open questions and sometimes crushing doubts that what I was pursuing had any meaning at all. I was on my own.

This book emerged from my experience of wandering in a kind of spiritual no-man's-land for many years after leaving organized religion and finding, at last, a spiritual home within. When you leave religion, you are not handed a guidebook for leading a sound spiritual life. If you are in that spiritual place, taking full responsibility for your soul and looking for guideposts, my story may help you navigate your way.

{ .. .. }

I believe we are waking up as a species. One sign of that grand awakening is the dawning awareness of our essential spiritual nature. Half a century ago, the mystic Pierre Teilhard de Chardin anticipated this new leap in consciousness when he said, "We have been thinking of ourselves as human beings on a spiritual journey—it would be more correct to think of ourselves as spiritual beings on a human journey."

Suddenly, it seems, many of us are feeling compelled to seek and have our own personal connection with our spiritual Source. We are making our own spiritual way in life apart from the compulsory dogmas, doctrines, and canons of organized religion. Every year, more and more of us are embarking on a spiritual search outside religion. From 1960 to 1980, the years during which I was struggling with the discrepancies between my religious faith and my evolving personal spiritual beliefs, Americans dropped out of organized religions in huge numbers: 84 percent of Jews, 69 percent of mainline Protestants, 61 percent of conservative Protestants, and 67 percent of Catholics.

In the past decade, 14.3 million Americans left organized religions, giving rise to the term "nones" for people who choose *none* on surveys of religious affiliation or preference. Of the nearly thirty million nones in total in America, less than one million think of themselves as atheists. This leaves approximately twenty-nine million Americans in search of a personal relationship with God, the Source, the Divinity, the Creator, the Great Spirit, the Supernatural Being, or whatever name they attach to a power higher than themselves, including the Higher Power. They are spiritual seekers.

Seeking spiritual truth and connection with the divine, however we conceive it, is part of being human. The pioneer psychotherapist Carl Gustav Jung and many others before and after him understood that spiritual seeking was a powerful theme in human nature. According to Jung, we all share a deep level of consciousness, which he called the collective unconsciousness—a pool of human experience and concepts that includes patterns of human thought or archetypes developed through the centuries. The Seeker is one of those archetypes.

So many of us, as we have seen, are being called to take full responsibility for the care of our souls by becoming spiritual seekers. This movement away from organized religion surely is part of a wider trend that touches many other areas of our lives. Probably the most well-documented is the parallel development taking place in the care of our bodies. The National Institutes of Health reports that in the United States 36 percent of us are using some form of complementary or alternative medicine (CAM). If megavitamin therapy is included in the definition of CAM, the figure rises to 62 percent.

Seekers of physical well-being are leaving conventional Western medicine, with its doctrinaire methods based solely on narrowly interpreted science, to pursue healing through alternative medical systems such as homeopathy, naturopathy, and ayurveda. Thirty years ago, alternative medical modalities were practically unheard of in the United States. Today, many thousands of people take up biologically based therapies, such as food supplements and herbs, along with chiropractic, osteopathy, energy healing, massage therapy, and acupuncture to address their health issues.

Spiritual seeking meets bodily healing in mind-body medicine, a variety of techniques designed to enhance the mind's ability to affect bodily function and symptoms. They include yoga, meditation, and other relaxation practices, and a range of spiritual practices.

What is happening in our relationship to the body—taking the primary responsibility for it away from "professionals"—is strikingly similar to what is unfolding in the realm of our spirituality. Just as we are seeking physical healing outside the old system of medicine we grew up with, we are also seeking to create a personal spiritual life away from the old structure of organized religion.

Many people in our culture find it difficult to recognize that there is a difference between religion and spirituality. Confusion around the two keeps sincere spiritual seekers in organized religion even when they know they are not being nourished by it. They often suspect, as I did, that continuing as a faithful member of a religious organization actually is impeding their spiritual progress. Nevertheless, they remain in religion because they believe it is the only way to have a relationship with their divine Source.

Religion offers us a connection with the divine—with conditions. Primary among those conditions, which include myriad laws regulating our conduct, is the notion that our relationship with our Source depends on the agency of a church and its ministers. In religion, we go to "God" through a paternal authority figure, a priest, minister, rabbi, preacher, guru, or some other form of spiritual specialist. The underlying assumption is that we are incapable of making and keeping a connection to our Source on our own. There is no room for spiritual seeking inside religion, because religion already has all the answers. In religion, what is required is faith.

Personal spirituality is entirely different from religiosity. Spirituality is the content of religion (or should be, under the best of circumstances). Spirituality is the awareness of ourselves as beings living in a multidimensional world, in connection with our Source and all other living beings. We know there is much more to us than what we can see and touch. This "much more" is the realm of spirit. We understand that our human experience is like an iceberg: only the tip, a small part of the whole, is visible. Living daily in this awareness, we lift all that is human in us to the level of interconnectedness with all other living things, all there is.

The challenge for the spiritual seeker is to come eventually to spiritually solid ground, avoiding the temptation to follow this self-important guru or that ego-inflated workshop leader, and sidestepping the sentimentality of most modern inspirational writers. The search for a meaningful personal spirituality is a serious one, demanding the full attention of both heart and mind.

Spiritual seekers create their own spiritual lives out of their personal experience of the divinity. They are led to build a personal spiritual philosophy—an open-minded, open-hearted, ever-evolving one—from many spiritual or humanistic traditions and worldviews. Some seekers are even guided back to all or part of the religion of their parents, but with a completely different spiritual understanding.

Out of personal spiritual philosophy, which motivates and gives meaning to all of our life, we live as "higher humans," beings with one foot on the earthly plane and the other in the mystical, unknown kingdom where we are one with all. From that awareness, we are moved to live our lives in a certain principled way—leading to service. The proof of a healthy spiritual life, I believe, is the extent to which we make ourselves available to the needs of others.

Many people remain members of an organized religion because they are concerned that without religion their children and family will receive no moral guidance. They may also be troubled about the prospect of being on their own spiritually, without a professional religious overseer or caretaker. If this or xix

a similar fear is keeping you tied to a set of religious beliefs that have ceased to nourish your soul, what follows should assure you that there is indeed life after religion.

If you have left organized religion and are searching for a way to create a rich spiritual life on your own, you will find here a plan for doing so, with my experience as an example. As a member of a Catholic religious order, I was as religious as one can get. Now, outside religion, I try to live a spiritually informed and inspired life, connected to my Source and to all that had its beginnings there.

When we become spiritual seekers, we take full responsibility for creating a deep personal bond with the divine on our own. The path may not be an easy one for some (it was not for me, at times), but the rewards of searching for the Source of all being and enjoying an intimate relationship with it are immense.

god on your own

PART ONE

beginning

CHAPTER ONE

a larger picture

Truth is within ourselves; it takes no rise
From outward things, whate'er you may believe.
—Robert Browning, "Paracelsus"

A few years ago, I took a meditation class with a small group of instructors at the college where I was teaching. The class, designed to reduce stress, met once a week for two hours. I was familiar with meditation from my earlier monastic experience, so generally I knew what to expect. For the first two weeks, everything I encountered was straightforward and somewhat predictable. Then, toward the end of the third class, something extraordinary happened.

As I sat on the floor cross-legged with my eyes closed, concentrating on my breathing, I felt myself pulling apart from my body and starting to float upward. My first feeling was a rush of anxiety, but then I worked through my fear of being separated from my body and the possibility that I might not be able to come back. Gradually, I relaxed into a pleasant feeling of weightlessness. I drifted up to the ceiling and slipped through the roof and into the night sky.

I was aware of myself as a large transparent ball, like a perfectly spherical soap bubble. There I was, flying through space. I found that I could fly fast and that I could maneuver myself in any direction. Right now, I decided to fly with tremendous speed toward a distant cool white light.

As I was flying, I looked to one side and saw another big bubble like myself. I flew to it and, to my surprise, merged with it—two bubbles in one. During this merging, I told a story to the other bubble. The story I told was the lifetime I was experiencing on earth. When I finished telling my story, the other bubble told me its story.

After I pulled away, I noticed there were other bubbles—millions of them—all flying at various speeds toward the far-off light. I flew over to one of those other bubbles, merged, and told my story again, this time remembering more of it and grasping more of its meaning.

At that point, the meditation class ended. With one long, deep breath, I was back in the room and back in my body. My colleagues ambled out of the room quietly and the instructor started closing up. Slowly, I moved out of my cross-legged position and stood up. My hand went to my face and wiped away a tear I did not remember shedding.

"We may be storytellers, then," I said to myself.

As I began writing this book, I remembered that fleeting vision, which could have been just a whimsical flight of my imagination or something more profound and more revealing, a window into eternity opening a crack during an otherwise perfectly ordinary exercise in stress reduction. Who we are may be storytellers. Why we are here may be to collect stories and share them with one another. These stories are the content of our lifetime.

From this vantage point in time, I am beginning to see the story I have been creating, with varying degrees of awareness, since I was born. Like your own story, probably, it has had its twists and turns, with more time than I would have liked spent in subplots and departures from the narrative. But those digressions aside, the theme of my story at least is beginning to emerge for me. I appear to have spent most of my life on a search for my spiritual self.

In this way as well, my story may be much the same as yours. I believe all of us are called to explore the world of spirit. When the call comes and how we go about our quest differs for each of us. But the impulse to venture beyond the narrow confines of our bodies into parts of us we cannot see or touch, yet know are there, appears to be an inherent human trait. You and I are seekers after spirit. We came into this world that way and we live our human lives, whether entirely conscious of it or not, deeply involved in a spiritual search.

Who are we, really? What are we doing here? Where did we come from? Where are we going? Are we more than our bodies? Did we live before we were born? Will we live again after we die? Why will we die? What happens to us after we die? These questions occur to all of us at one time or another during our lives.

In asking them, we begin to push the physical envelope that we know well and move into spiritual territory, about which we still know little but to which we are irresistibly drawn.

Traditionally, many of us have sought answers to these and perhaps a hundred more spiritual questions in organized religion. We went to churches, synagogues, mosque, temples, and ashrams to try to learn something about our purpose here on earth and about a grander plan in the world, if any, and how one might relate to the other. Beyond our questions, we were looking to satisfy that deep, passionate yearning we all feel for a connection to a world beyond the limitations of the physical.

For some of us, the answers we received from religion were inadequate or not answers at all. Instead, religion offered us a set of beliefs about spirituality to which we should subscribe "on faith." Even though we felt spiritually undernourished by organized religion, we might have stayed with it and tried to make it work for ourselves. Or we might simply have given up on the possibility of having a meaningful spiritual life, resigning ourselves to wander forever in a spiritless twilight zone.

However, you and I do have other choices, and that is what this book is about. You absolutely can have a satisfying and meaningful spiritual life outside religion. Seeking for your personal spiritual identity is your birthright. You can move out of the confines of a religious system if it is not furthering your spiritual life; you can free yourself to explore the great human questions, and you can be successful in that sacred endeavor.

This is a fascinating time of transition and transformation. One of the many areas of our life experiencing fundamental change is how we approach our relationship to our divine

Source. Willingness to experiment with spiritual searching has come into the cultural mainstream, giving rise to the term "cafeteria religions," where people choose their religious beliefs and practices according to what inspires and nourishes them.

Our religious landscape at this exciting time in human evolution is vast and varied. You may be a member in good standing of an organized religion and regularly attend church or temple. Or you may consider yourself to have a religious affiliation— Methodist, Presbyterian, Roman Catholic, Baptist, and so on— but do not practice your religion often. Maybe you attend services more or less regularly at quasi-religious organizations such as Unity or Religious Science but regard traditional religions as too limiting for your taste. You might have a cultural connection with a religion, but little else.

On the other hand, you may never have been associated with a religion. In the 1960s, when all the established religions in the United States (and in many other parts of the world) experienced a sudden hemorrhage of membership, the people who left the religion of their parents and grandparents typically reared their children outside religion. You may be a member of that generation of the religionless, just now navigating your way along a personal spiritual path with few guideposts to help.

If you are like millions of us at this moment in history, you may have more than one of these scenarios running inside you. You could be culturally devoted to Judaism, for instance, enjoying certain music, dances, foods, and traditions but at the same time finding that its core beliefs and rituals have little or no meaning to your day-to-day life. You may appreciate Islamic customs and manners, with their elaborate emphasis on hospitality and respect, but stay away from a mosque because the religious beliefs behind those customs do not inspire you. Or you might feel drawn to the philosophy of a Catholic saint such as Francis of Assisi, but not to practice Catholicism because you are not interested in following the doctrines and proscriptions of the Catholic Church.

When Pope John Paul II died in 2005, hundreds of thousands descended upon Rome to pay their last respects. At Saint Peter's Basilica, they waited in long lines night and day through all kinds of weather to view his body and say good-bye. But when the mourners were interviewed about why they had made such a heroic effort to be there, many said they were not Catholic. Others who were Catholic said they did not agree with the church's doctrines on birth control, abortion, gay rights, and a range of other social issues. They had come to Rome to honor John Paul's moral courage and humanitarianism. They admired his dedication to his own personal spiritual path.

Like those sincere pilgrims to Rome, you may feel that you have one foot in and one foot out of organized religion. No matter where you are on this spectrum of possibilities, however, religion is an issue for you. It is not a concern for you alone, since where you stand on religion influences your relationships with the people in your life in essential ways. You may be troubled to think that in the absence of religion your children, or the children of others, would receive no moral guidance; that is enough for many dedicated parents to stay uncomfortably, even intolerably, in a religion. You may fear that if you sever your religious affiliation you will destroy a precious bond with your parents, aunts, uncles, and cousins—your family support structure.

Sometimes, the prospect of being on your own spiritually appears daunting, or worse, risky, or downright dangerous. If you are contemplating leaving your religion or have done so, you may be experiencing anxiety, anger, grief, or shame over it. These emotions are common to everyone who has left a religion. I have felt all of them at times in my own process, but even if they are typical and expected while we are feeling them, they can be enormously disturbing.

I have traveled in the sometimes-hard terrain between organized religion and personal spirituality. I know what it is like to wander in a spiritual no-man's-land. I also know what peace of mind, joy, and sense of connection lies at the destination of spiritual striving. In these pages, I offer you the story of that journey, as told by one big bubble to another.

{ .. .. }

My experience with the realm of spirit began long before I entered a monastery. It happened out of nowhere when I was seven or eight years old. I was playing a game of tag with the other children in the neighborhood, running around on the lawn of my grandparents' house. Suddenly, the other children were gone and I was alone, or so it seemed to me. Something welled up from deep within me. Even now, after all these years of remembering that moment and reflecting on it, I find it difficult to describe the feeling. A wave of joy rose from my solar plexus and filled my body completely. Time stopped. I felt sheer bliss. I was utterly filled and finished.

In that ecstatic moment, my consciousness seemed to take a wild leap upward. I knew there was another world I had never imagined existed, and I felt perfectly at home in it. For days after my blissful moment, I tried to recreate the feeling, but without success. Instead of getting the feeling back, I began to sense a vague tug at my heart to venture forth and explore. My business-as-usual childhood was over.

"There is always one moment in childhood when the door opens and lets the future in," Deepak Chopra has written. You may remember something like that happening to you during your childhood or at another stage in your life. These experiences might have come on spontaneously, as mine did, or some outside event could have triggered them. We all respond differently to these brief openings into another reality, but I believe we all have experienced them at one time or another. My response was to consider it a kind of call. Little did I know at the time that a momentary break while playing a children's game of tag would lead me, a decade later, to the gates of a monastery.

Our family was Catholic, but not unusually so. We observed the ordinary daily lives of Catholics: meatless Fridays, Confession on Saturdays, Mass on Sundays. By the time I got to Catholic high school, I was familiar with the concept of a religious vocation—how it meant "a calling from God," and how this is what priests and nuns experienced that directed them into their profession. If a vocation is a feeling deep within that cannot be denied or avoided, then sometime in the middle of the twelfth grade I knew had a vocation.

I applied for entrance to the Congregation of Holy Cross, an order of teaching brothers or monks, and was accepted. Our parish priest volunteered to drive me from my home in Ohio to the congregation's postulancy in Wisconsin. Early one muggy

June morning, a week after high school graduation, his black Buick pulled up into our driveway. Inside the house, my sleep-deprived mother sniffed back her tears. She had spent much of the night packing my footlocker, and folding in love notes for me to find when I unpacked. I walked out of the house and into the car—the shortest imaginable distance that was also the unfathomable space between two worlds.

When I entered monastic life, I embarked on a path to becoming a professional religious man. Like others before me who had chosen that profession in a tradition stretching back centuries, I wore the contemporary garb of a "religious," black with a Roman collar, which identified me in public and set me apart.

Along with my brothers, I practiced the Catholic religion to the letter: attendance at Mass every morning, recitation of daily prayers, litanies, devotions, the rosary, the sacraments, and so on. In fact, being a professional religious meant I was living what our master of novices would say was "the fullness of religion." Catholics outside the cloister did as much as they could to live the faith, he explained, but there were always the distractions of lay life—relationships, children, jobs, and all the obligations that went with them. We who were professional religious were kind of prototype Catholics, models of what it meant to live our religion truly and completely.

Within the walls of the monastery, my life was not much different from the life of a monk in Europe during the Middle Ages. I was part of a community of about sixty monks, ranging in age from eighteen, like me, to eighty. The monastery was self-sufficient. We grew our own food in the fields around the monastery, which was in a remote farming area in the Midwest. Our life was exceedingly simple. We wore plain clothing, ate humble meals, and at night retired to small individual rooms furnished only with a bed, a sink, and a desk and chair for read- ing and for study. We rose before dawn to chant prayers and went to sleep in the early evening, after meditation. Except for rare occasions, we observed the rule of silence.

All the monks living in my monastery took vows of poverty, chastity, and obedience. Under the vow of poverty, we gave up personal ownership of all material things; everyone owned everything in common. The intent of the vow was to foster detachment from possessions. The vow of chastity meant we abstained from sensual pleasure and remained celibate and outside of relationship with another person.

Obedience was the surrender of our personal will to the needs of the community, articulated by the monastery's chief administrator, the abbot. The vow of obedience dictated where we would live—at this monastery or another affiliated one—and what tasks we would perform. We might be assigned to work in the kitchen or the garden, or given the job of porter (taking care of visitors), regulator (supervising the daily schedule), apothe- cary (looking after the physical health of the other monks), or extern (going outside the monastery to obtain special items or services). One of my favorite "obediences," as they were called, was reader—reading aloud from inspirational books in the monastery refectory during our silent meals.

The practice of obedience became a somewhat larger issue as the years went on. At a moment's notice, we might be sent to another of the order's monastic houses to carry out an assign-

ment there. We would pack one small bag and hurry to the next
religious house to become part of that established community
of monks. The process of being uprooted and replanted served
several purposes. One was to fill the needs of the greater community, of course, but the more spiritual aspect had to do with
detachment—giving us still another opportunity to surrender
the comforts of familiarity.

Poverty, chastity, and obedience formed the foundation of
our monastic way of life. The objective was to be free to concentrate completely on the life of the spirit without allowing anything to interfere. The three vows were sacred promises we made
to God, not to the Catholic Church or to the monastery. So serious was the commitment to the vows, monks new to monastic
life took them only for a year at a time for three years. After
those three years, monks could opt to extend their trial period
for another three consecutive years before pronouncing "perpetual vows." Taking the vows was a grave matter.

Being a monk was not easy. We lived apart from the world
not only geographically but also emotionally and mentally. In
our monastery, there were no radios, televisions, newspapers,
magazines—anything that might distract us from our focus on
the inner life. A telephone, in the abbot's office, connected us
marginally with the outside world. Although we lived in community, the rule of silence and the restriction on forming "particular friendships" distanced us from one another, leaving us
with an aching loneliness even amid a large group of men.

Many of the brothers, craving more intimate human connections or fewer constraints on their freedom, left monastic life
and returned home during the first or second year. It was just too

much. But I stayed behind the walls, looking for answers to spiritual questions I seemed to have been asking since that remarkable afternoon of my childhood. Spirituality was what I aspired to; for me, the fullness of religion was the means to that end.

{ .. .. }

Historically, the methods we humans have followed to explore our spiritual dimension are varied almost beyond belief, from murmuring prayers on a string of beads to ritually murdering each other on an altar of sacrifice. We have starved and mutilated ourselves, or stuffed and drugged ourselves, trying to connect to the realm of spirit. We have investigated our spiritual nature within groups—in tribes with unique identity, such as "the chosen people" or "the elect"—and individually, as mystics, mediums, saints, and shamans.

Through it all, we have become attached to a few interesting notions. One is that the spiritual world exists far outside the earthly world we can see and experience. Another is that the world of spirit, ruled by an all-powerful divinity, is separate and apart from us, making any kind of association extremely difficult. Still another is that access to the spiritual realm depends on a middle-person whose job it is to take us to the other world, usually through a process that involves making us worthy to enter it.

We invented religion to house these notions and many more. With its rituals, ceremonies, and other formal procedures, religion was the way we thought we could get a glimpse into our own spiritual nature. Of course, owing to our fundamentally unworthy condition (or so went our core mind-set), we would have to submit to the rules of religion, administered by a priest caste, and commit to its system of beliefs, which we would have to take on faith as truth.

"Religion starts with the perception that something is wrong," writes Karen Armstrong in *The History of God.* We believe we came into this world flawed, and we must spend the rest of our lives making up for that original imperfection. Only religion, with its elaborate formulas and stipulations, can lift us out of our faulty nature and reform us to the point where we can have access to the spiritual realm.

Eventually, we institutionalized religion and made it one of the pillars of civilization, alongside education, government, medicine, commerce, and so on. Religion was, and is now, organized much like a corporation, with a hierarchy of command, a structure for getting things done more or less efficiently, employees, a body of beliefs and ideological viewpoints, a "product" (connection to the divine and the world of spirit), and a recognizable character and "culture."

For a long time—eons, really—we had the idea that religion was the only way to explore our spiritual selves. For us, religion provided the path that would lead us to fulfill the burning desire within to engage the great human questions, which are spiritual questions.

We found organized religion tremendously useful as an answerer of questions. Without skipping a beat, it gives us definitive responses to thorny, enigmatic questions. "Why did God make you?" asks the Catholic catechism. "God made me to know Him, to love Him, and to serve Him in this world, and to be happy with Him forever in heaven . . ." comes the instant reply. Never mind that the answer to one question leads to other questions, and then more questions, until we understand that the spiral of questions and answers stops only when we accept the whole package with a leap of faith. Still, any answer is more of a comfort than no answer at all.

In time, many kinds of religion arose that were based on local languages, customs, traditions, and worldviews. All of them were organized similarly, with hierarchies, priesthoods, sacred scriptures, rituals, and the other characteristics of religion. However, each of them also rested on the principle that it and it alone was the authentic religion: my God was the true God.

Because religion was one of the mainstays of society, along with government, education, the military, and the rest, religious animosities most often expressed themselves in political terms, ending with wars. This was cruelly ironic, since every religion's fundamental belief was that the individual person was a reflection of the divine creator, and therefore sacred; in all the religions, killing another human being was strictly forbidden. Still, over the centuries we slaughtered one another by the millions upon millions in the name of "God" and the sacredness of life.

This alone should have made us suspicious of organized religion. Far from furnishing spiritual sustenance for their believers, the various religions actually seemed to be undermining personal spirituality by coercing us into peculiarly unspiritual behaviors. Instead of bringing us together with our divine Source, religion was separating us from it and from each other by ever-widening chasms.

Many people stayed in a religion even when they knew in their heart that the system they were in was not fostering their spiritual potential. Try as they might, sincerely following all the rules, they sensed there was much more to spiritual exploration than religion offered them.

In the past, it was dangerous to harbor these thoughts. If you told someone about your religious misgivings you could be ostracized—or worse, tortured and even put to death. Better to stay put, make peace with religion, and hope for the best. No inquisitor could see into your heart to find your true feelings.

We believed religion was the only way to approach the world of spirit; if we were left unsatisfied at the table of organized religion, feeling that it did not answer our questions and even discouraged or prevented further inquiry, we had no choice but to go into a kind of religious self-exile. We thought it was a choice between sticking with religion, which did not nourish our spiritual strivings, or leaving it and denying ourselves the possibility of pursuing a spiritual life altogether.

Now we know there are other ways. We have another set of choices. We certainly can leave the religion of our parents and grandparents to create a personal spirituality on our own. We can follow that path to seek our highest human potential. Our search for spirituality may start in religion, but it may be just the prologue of our spiritual story.

My own spiritual seeking began in religion, from perhaps an extreme expression of it—eight years living a monastic life as a professional religious man. At the beginning of my monastic journey, I was convinced there was no other way to pursue my compelling call to seek my spiritual self. In fact, by the conventions of that time there were few alternatives if any. I expected to be a monk forever; I had taken perpetual vows. But things turned out differently. Paradoxically, perhaps, my spiritual search, which

I had assumed would be fulfilled in monastic life, led me out of the monastery and eventually out of religion entirely.

If you are sensing that organized religion is not a workable spiritual path, you are not alone. I believe you and I are part a planetary movement, a fraternity of seekers around the world who, by the millions, are awakening to a new way of connecting to their spiritual Source.

We are being encouraged to do this by the nature of the times. Many modern thinkers are saying we are in the midst of a great transformation in how we envision ourselves and the world around us. Think of it as a turning point for our planet. Taking responsibility for the health of our selves—our whole being, body, mind, emotions, and soul—by creating a personal spiritual life is part of this larger picture.

In 1962, Thomas Kuhn's *The Structure of Scientific Revolutions* popularized the concept of "paradigm shift," in which "one conceptual world-view is replaced by another." Kuhn was speaking about fundamental patterns of ideas in science, but recently the paradigm-shift approach to human evolution has been extended by many to include how we regard everything in our human experience. We go along for a time with a certain set of inner pictures of who and where we are, and then suddenly there is a change as the familiar set of pictures is replaced by another.

The tricky thing about a paradigm shift is that we can perceive it only through our rearview mirror. Once a shift has occurred, we can see how we are now and how we were then and compare the two. While the shift is in progress, though, we may feel we are on slippery ground. Nevertheless, living through a paradigm shift can be tremendously exhilarating.

Whenever we try to imagine what could be waiting for us at the other end of the impending paradigm shift, we invariably come up blank. People of the fifteenth century could not imagine a world that was not flat. Like them, we find it difficult to picture a human existence with ten dimensions, a physical body that can be redesigned moment to moment by our thinking or feeling, or a material world we are collectively creating from light.

It is as impossible for us to entertain the concept that time may not exist, for instance, as it was for a person in the Middle Ages to grasp the "absurdity," as Robert Cardinal Bellarmine called it in 1615 during the trial of Galileo, of the earth flying through space. To counter the assertion, the cardinal offered the logical observation that if the earth were moving the tops of all the trees in the world would be bent from the force of the unremitting wind.

None of the possible scenarios we can dream up may have anything to do with the shift that is upon us. In spite of the difficulty of picturing something that has not happened yet, we are receiving some inkling of what a new worldview would look like.

In the realm of spirituality, the shift may have several aspects. One is a turning away from owning the spiritual truth of another or of a tradition, and going toward discovering spiritual truth on our own, by personal experience. The old paradigm would have us believe the "inspired revelations" contained in a sacred book, for instance, are the truth about spirit, and if we live according to its precepts and proscriptions we will have connection with our Source. The new paradigm suggests that we can have direct experience of and connection with our Source, without holy texts, dogmas, or priestly transactions. In fact, because these things assert final truth, they may actually inhibit or prevent our personal seeking.

Another feature of the shift is related to this. We will be asked to take personal responsibility for our actions, thoughts, and beliefs. In the past, we might act on an article of our religious faith that went against our conscience. Under the new paradigm, such a thing would be unthinkable. Our inner guidance will be the arbiter of our values and the deeds springing from them.

A new way of seeing ourselves and one another awaits us at the other side of the approaching shift. The spiritual principle of oneness will dominate, giving all areas of the spiritual realm a humanitarian character.

Your spiritual life, like the spiritual lives of many millions of us, may have begun in organized religion, but it does not have to end there. In the future, we may well look back to see that religion has been our spiritual nursery. Now that we are maturing as a species, a dazzling new spiritual world awaits us.

CHAPTER TWO

beyond religion

There are in our existence spots of time,
Which with distinct preeminence retain
A renovating virtue. . . .
—WILLIAM WORDSWORTH, *THE PRELUDE*

A CRISP AUTUMN afternoon in the heart of rural Indiana. Outside in a cloister courtyard, the sun spreads itself on spent rose bushes like butter. The sweet scents of cornhusks and apples are in the air. In the distance, long stretches of recently harvested fields, a tractor turning over furrows for fall planting. In one corner of the cloister, drying rust-colored leaves from a stately maple rasp against the enormous window of the monastery classroom. If you were an artist and wanted to paint a picture of an almost otherworldly peacefulness and tranquility, you would set up your easel right there.

When I try to locate exactly at what time, during my monastic sojourn, I began to feel uneasy about my religious beliefs I go back in my mind to this serene setting. A seed was planted in my heart that afternoon. Years later, it would sprout into a completely new spiritual awareness.

All the important phases of our life start at a turning point—something someone says to us, something we read, somewhere we visit, or some sudden inspiration that comes out of nowhere. The turning point may be insignificant to us at the time, but looking back we see that it carries tremendous power to steer us in another direction. Once on our new course, everything that went before may look like a detour.

A monk leads a life not only of work and prayer but of study as well. At our monastery, afternoons in fall and winter were devoted to rigorous instruction in theology. On that crisp autumn day, as I listened to one of our theology teachers, a visiting Dominican monk, I began to feel roiling impatience cooking up in me. The topic of the lecture was the famous Five Proofs for the Existence of God, a pyrotechnic display of Aristotelian logic from the thirteenth-century work of Saint Thomas Aquinas, a Dominican predecessor of our teacher.

"God's existence," he was saying, quoting Thomas's *Summa Theologica*, "can be proved in five ways. The first and most obvious way is based on the existence of motion."

For most of the class, I tried to figure out where my feelings of irritation were coming from. Usually, I liked heady intellectual discourses such as what the theologian was giving; the beliefs of my religion came alive for me when presented in a way that made good sense. I watched the learned lecturer as he dashed words onto the blackboard, oblivious to the chalk dust accumulating on the edges of his black cape, and listened to the proofs of God's existence.

"Whatever is moved must be moved by something else. This cannot continue to infinity, however, for if it did there would be no first mover and consequently no other movers, because these other movers are such only insofar as they are moved by a first mover."

He went on. "God is the prime mover of all things, the first cause, a rational necessity, the standard of perfection, the creator of a first pattern."

At last, it hit me. The reason for the mounting anger and anxiety in the pit of my stomach was not the logic, which was exasperatingly airtight, but the whole concept of approaching the subject of God in this way. I was being given other people's answers for a question that, in my mind and heart, required no answer. This spiritual issue—the king of all issues, the existence of God—asked only for contemplation. I could feel the lecturer's cold exercise in logic putting distance between God and me, and the distance was growing with every passing minute. My religion had begun to separate me from my personal urge to seek my creative Source.

The God of my childhood was an Old Man with a long white beard who lived in the sky above the clouds and rewarded us for our right actions or punished us for wrong actions. In my teen years, I began to reimagine God as a more beneficent, but still remote Person who lived in the far reaches of space. By the time I entered monastic life, I was reimagining God again, this time as a Presence that was pleased when His (God was still male) creations cared for one another.

Beyond Religion

Four years earlier, entering monasticism, I had given my life to that God, to serve by teaching and by offering myself as an example of a life motivated by religion. Now, as the novelty of the monastic way began to wear off, I was seeing the extent of my commitment. If the rest of my life were going to be an unbroken string of days arranged around the same unvarying austere routine, I wanted to envision a more personal God. I would need that to sustain me through the difficult times.

Theology was the repository of my religious beliefs, the structure on which rested my relationship to God and God's relationship to me. But the structure of my religion, designed to bring me closer to my Source, seemed to be creating an unbridgeable gulf between the God I longed to know and to serve and me.

I suppose the issue under all this was that I felt uncomfortable with being told what to believe. Other people's truths were theirs, not necessarily mine. In my evolving sense of spirituality, I was yearning for a set of truths I could espouse out of my own experience.

From this autumn afternoon on, my inner life was in turmoil. A week later, when I finally had the courage to speak to my spiritual director about my nagging doubts and frustrations, he said they were perfectly normal feelings. He himself had experienced similar reservations but overcame them in time with faith. He suggested I pray over it and ask for more faith to handle the crisis.

For months I tried, but the more faith I applied to my misgivings the farther away my Source seemed to recede, leaving me abandoned on a heap of spiritual wishful thinking, confusion, and denial. Eventually, I would have to face the fact that religion was not working for me.

So on an idyllic autumn afternoon in a monastery cloister, in the middle of a lecture on the existence of God given by a theological expert, the most unexpected thing happened: I began to lose my faith. Much later, I would come to see that I had also begun to *find* something that afternoon: a new path to the adventure of seeking my spiritual self on my own. But first, much wandering in a spiritual maze awaited me.

You probably have your own turning point, or several of them, in your personal spiritual history. During a sermon in church or temple, you began to question an article of faith and over time a single question started the dominoes falling. Or a friend asked you to explain why you perform some ritual or mutter some prayer; you could not come up with an appropriate answer and the episode triggered a string of doubts waiting in the back of your mind for the day when they could be expressed.

However you encountered your own turning point, something undoubtedly caused you to begin looking at your relationship to religion in another way. It set in motion a series of thoughts, emotions, and actions that led eventually to your leaving organized religion.

{ .. .. }

I have found there is a process to leaving religion not unlike the process psychiatrist Elizabeth Kübler-Ross outlined for dying. A kind of death is taking place, after all: the death of long-held beliefs and values, the death of the God of childhood, even the death of familiar spiritual illusions and fantasies. The process applies equally to those of us who have left religion, believers who are losing their commitment to religion, and even to those who have never officially practiced a religion but have inherited religious sensibilities from their parents or grandparents.

In 1969, Kübler-Ross wrote in her classic *On Death and Dying* about a pattern that people confronting death commonly follow. She called the pattern the stages of dying. The first stage is *denial and isolation.* She found that almost all terminally ill patients began here, usually reacting to a negative medical verdict. "It's not true." Even if it is true, they deny it by isolating themselves from others who may want to confirm the truth.

Second is *anger,* which can be expressed in many ways, especially projecting it onto people and things (doctors, nurses, family members, improper nutrition, tobacco, an accident, and most of all God). Passive-aggressive behavior also falls under this category, first going along with something but then lashing out inappropriately.

The third stage of the dying process is *bargaining.* In this stage, thinking that if God did not respond to anger then maybe promising to be good will be effective. Next comes *depression,* mourning the loss of health, mobility, friends, future aspirations, all the things, good and bad, in life.

Finally is the stage of *acceptance.* Kübler-Ross makes it clear that this is not a happy stage, even if it suggests peace of mind; in fact, it is usually devoid of feelings. Acceptance is surrender to the inevitable and unavoidable. Although these stages are believed to be universal, not everyone goes through each stage and the order may differ from one person to the next.

Some people leave religion in a snap, by simply not going to church or synagogue another time. Though they may have been thinking things over for ages, their decision to end it all appears impulsive. Others take longer, maybe months or years longer, trying to balance both their loyalty to religion and their disenchantment with it. But no matter how long it takes, the process of leaving could be the same for everyone.

To follow Kübler-Ross's formula, the first stage for you may be to deny there is even a problem with your religion. A nagging doubt exists, the suspicion that you are wasting your time with something that is not nourishing you, but you refuse to believe it. Some of your denial may come from the huge investment made up to that point—an emotional, mental, and spiritual investment. I lingered in this step for four years; in my monastic commitment, I had a great deal invested. Isolation is part of this denial, staying away from people or things that support the painful doubts we are experiencing.

Anger against religion is quite common. These days, it is considered impolite to vent anger against religion in public, but in a safe small group you are likely to hear some anger expressed. Sometimes the anger is turned inward at oneself for feeling disappointed with religion. A man in my hometown stayed in this stage for the last thirty years of his life because he was mad at God for allowing the illness and death of his wife. He died still steeped in his anger, leaving explicit instructions that he was not to be given a church service and his body was not to be buried in a consecrated cemetery plot. He told his family he had chosen hell over a heartless God. Admittedly, his was an extreme case, but you may have similar stories to tell about people who shake their fist in rage at heaven.

We do not know much about the bargaining stage, because it usually takes place as an inner dialogue between us and the

God of our religion. With me, this was the point at which I promised to be a perfect monk if only my reservations and misgivings passed away. I lived monasticism as impeccably as I could, but the uncertainties remained.

Depression sets in after going through the preceding stages of facing the death of religion in us. This is another area where many people stay, sometimes for years. You know how you feel when you are depressed; you are tired most of the time, you do not eat properly (too much or too little), you are inactive and listless. Leaving religion, you may find these depressed feelings are about mourning over the past, a time when you had no questions or reservations.

This is also the time when the real sense of loss sets in. If your religion has provided you with a social outlet, getting you out of the house and together with people, you may need to mourn the loss and feel unhappy over the prospect of finding new social expressions. If you found comfort in your religion's belief system, a body of doctrines that conveniently held all the answers to the big questions of life, you may drift into despondency mulling over the gargantuan task of building new beliefs on your own.

At last, we accept the inescapable conclusion that religion does not work for us, and for the sake of our spiritual growth we must move on. As in the process of dying, this stage is not exactly happy, but rather resigned. I do not know of anyone who really takes pleasure in leaving religion. One reason is that when we leave the religion of our childhood, we also leave behind a large piece of family history and tradition based on shared spiritual experience. For some of us, this stage in the process is a flat-feeling place where an important part of our lives goes away, but nothing comes in to replace it.

Do you recognize any of these stages in your own process? Kübler-Ross reminds us they are archetypal or universal progressions in the course of dying; not everyone experiences all of them, and not everyone goes through them in the order in which she presents them. You may be interested in charting out your process to see how it connects with her outline. Simply knowing there is a process to leaving religion, and that many people are doing it at this important time in human evolution, can give us some comfort on an otherwise uncomfortable journey.

{ .. .. }

Some of the obstacles you encounter in going from having a religion to not having one do not seem to be part of a process but belong to a general sense of dislocation. One is doubt— about your religious beliefs, certainly, but also about whether you should leave your religion because of those misgivings. At a certain point in evolving out of religion toward a personal spirituality, "Am I doing the right thing?" becomes an urgent question.

First, there is doubt about what you truly believe. If you find some of your religion's spiritual "truths" difficult to get your head and heart around, you have to strike out on your own to try to resolve your concerns. In most organized faiths, doubt is considered a fundamental fault that some call a sin. This makes sense, when you think about it, since faith and doubt are at opposite ends of the spiritual spectrum. Religion depends entirely on a person's belief in doctrines that it considers self-evident. To doubt any or all of those creeds goes to the heart of the believer's religious connection.

For Christian religions, the unacceptability of doubt is included in the Bible. The New Testament story about the Apostle Thomas makes the point that belief is paramount to religion. Jesus has risen from the dead, but Thomas, who has just heard about the miracle, says he will not believe it unless he can touch the wounds of the crucified master. Jesus appears in the room and invites Thomas to examine the wounds in his hands and his side. Thomas does so and proclaims his belief. Then comes the lesson for Thomas and the rest of us. Jesus is made to say, "Blessed are those who have not seen, and yet believe." Blind faith, apparently, is a blessing.

The story of Doubting Thomas is told in the Gospel according to John, which was among the last of the Christian scriptures to be written. At the time of its authorship, around 100 A.D., Christianity had separated itself from Judaism and was seeking its own distinct identity, and to increase its numbers. Many Biblical scholars think the Thomas tale was included in the Gospel as a way for the early church to build a loyal following.

Other religions appear to tolerate doubt as a means to the end of dedicating oneself more solidly to the faith. It is thought of as part of the process of truly believing—a phase, like childhood—and therefore allowed. But doubt cannot go on forever. At some point, sooner rather than later, one is asked to make a commitment to the body of beliefs in question. Organized religion would not survive for long if it encouraged endless doubt in its adherents.

Uncertainty over religious beliefs is one thing. Uncertainty about whether to face the situation and stay in a religion or leave it is quite another. When this comes up, the natural inclination is to take it to a spiritual advisor or counselor, but if the person is a minister of the very religion you are contemplating leaving, then you probably will not get the answers you need. Instead, you are apt to encounter a persuasive argument to hold on to your religious connection, which is only natural. Family and friends may not be helpful in this regard either, for the same reasons: they are probably clinging to the old religious beliefs for a host of motives of their own and would be unwilling to compromise them by much discussion with a doubter.

Doubt is a particularly shady issue; it clouds our thinking and keeps us in a state of paralysis. Because we doubt whether we should stay in an organized religion or go forward into unknown spiritual territory, we remain where we are—often for years. With doubt, a kind of spiritual weariness sets in. Instead of feeling excitement over exploring the big questions of life, we settle for the stale and slanted answers of other people passed down through the ages. We endure our affiliation with religion. Fear keeps a doubter in the pews as well. But fear of what? After I left monastic life, I continued a friendship with one of the brothers who had also left the order. Though we lived in different parts of the country, our paths would cross from time to time. Once, having dinner together, he confided to me that although he had given up his monk's vows and his Catholic religion long ago, he still harbored a fear that would not go away. Then he told me something that in the moment made absolutely no sense. In fact, I thought he was joking. But for him, it was no joke. He leaned toward me as a penitent would in a confessional and said, "I'm afraid of going to hell."

32

Hell had not been a reality for him since he left the monastery and the faith. In fact, he said, even as a child he always thought the literal hell where people burned forever was just a figment of the religious imagination. Nevertheless, here he was, a grown man, admitting his worst fear to me. Of course, hell can be a metaphor for the bad times that we encounter in life; we say we are going through hell. However, it was not fear of the metaphorical hell that haunted my good friend.

Hell is an archetype, an inherited idea about eternal punishment existing in the collective unconscious of all humans. When we were born onto the human scene, hell (or whatever it is called in other religious traditions) came with it. As much as we try to dismiss deeply held universal images like this, we can go only so far. Apparently something stays in the back of the mind, especially if the notion was active in childhood, when we formed our first inner pictures of the world.

Whether the literal hell or the figurative one, fear of some kind of spiritual punishment can prevent you from venturing out on your own spiritual wings. This is a problem each of us must face and solve on our own. A first step is to acknowledge that religious conditioning added to a collective concept can be a powerful roadblock on the way to spiritual freedom. The rest is to come to your own understanding of what hell might mean. Later, when you are building your own personal spirituality, you can decide whether hell, whatever form it takes, has a place in it or not.

Other fears may arise as you make the transition out of organized religion. The process of leaving is often stalled or even stopped by concern over being ostracized from family, friends, and believers who are still in the fold. This is a particularly chilling issue in some of the major religions. Sometimes people who turn their back on their faith are shunned, scorned, even considered "dead" by their religious group. The prospect of being disowned by the tribe is so compelling that it keeps some people in religion long after it has any meaning for them. We are human, after all.

Shame, disgrace, and embarrassment go with this social aspect of leaving religion. When I was thinking of leaving monastic life after eight years, I felt a tremendous embarrassment about returning to my hometown a failure. It was not the first consideration in my decision to prolong my stay in the monastery, but what I perceived as public humiliation surely factored into it.

You may encounter a similar sense of shame over leaving religion. For some, this is not a problem at all; for others, it is a difficult hurdle. Much depends on how deeply your religious beliefs are rooted in shame itself. If disgrace and humiliation were important underlying components of your faith (as in all of the sin-based religious systems), you would likely feel the pain of embarrassment more keenly and it might be acute enough to keep you from leaving. How attached you have been to your religious social circle can also determine the extent of your shame. You may be not only a believer in church doctrines but also an active participant in ancillary church activities. Leaving those important human connections behind can cause shame to well up and influence if, how, and when you leave your religion.

Some of us may never get over the guilt that invariably accompanies leaving the religion of our childhood. Years passed before I could say to someone, "I am not a Catholic." Even now, I find it difficult to identify myself as a former (or in that religion's words, fallen-away) Catholic. Later in this book, I suggest how you might return to your religion of origin but with vastly different spiritual views—and without shame. For now, though, simply acknowledging these feelings may help to disperse them as you walk a path to a new spiritual realm.

Finally, and maybe most important, the prospect of a bleak future after leaving your religion might be an obstacle to moving on. A sense of spiritual void, barren and joyless, looms on the horizon. You may foresee a long and lonely road ahead of you, with no help and no hope of finding a home for your spiritual longings. You may have the sinking feeling that if you give up your religion you will give up all possibility of having a connection with your creative Source.

Rest assured, there is a full and rich spiritual life after religion. Indeed, your true life of the spirit may be awaiting you beyond the limitations of doctrines and proscriptions, in the freedom to explore the magnificent vistas of a personal spiritual vision.

{ .. .. }

I believe there is such a thing as grace. We think of grace in the context of religious belief, of course, but it belongs to all spiritual paths, in or out of religion. Grace is unmerited assistance that comes to us from a high spiritual place. It gets us unstuck and pushes us forward. I have known grace to operate in my life many times over in the most amazing of circumstances. You also have felt grace enter your life and work its magic.

Grace supports our sincere desire to follow our conscience (which itself is a spark from the divine fire) and pursue a path of authentic spirituality. If we are stalled in our process of leaving religion and finding another way, we must remember that grace works in us and for us.

You do not have to wait for grace to descend upon you. You can call on it, and ask for the boost you need to get you up to the next step in your spiritual evolution. Sometimes grace comes in the form of another person, or as a special opportunity. Frequently it arrives on the heels of a synchronicity, a seemingly coincidental occurrence such as thinking about someone and then a moment later running into the person on the street, or entertaining a question and someone phones you with the answer.

At a special time of anguish over my religious commitment, grace appeared to me in the form of a frayed, dog-eared paperback. One bitterly cold January morning toward the end of my eight years in the monastery, a snow-dusted box of books arrived at our order's Scholasticate from one of our religious houses at Notre Dame. The Scholasticate was another step in the process of becoming a full teaching monk, university training coupled with strict observance of our monastic rule. In the middle of a particularly harsh winter, the sense of icy desolation that had descended on me in the two years since I began to question my faith was about to melt.

The box came just in time. I had been in a spiritual limbo for months, agonizing over my commitment to monastic life and my religion. Applying prayer and faith to the situation, as my spiritual director advised, did nothing but compound the problem. I wanted to explore my personal connection to my divine Source without the constraints and pat answers of religious dogma.

Help was at the bottom of that box, in a fascinating book called *The Phenomenon of Man,* written by a French Jesuit priest and paleontologist, Pierre Teilhard de Chardin, in the 1950s. It was either carelessly included or intentionally smuggled into the Scholasticate from the outside. The Vatican's Congregation for the Doctrine of the Faith was investigating the author to see if his writings contained heresy. These musings of a priest-scientist, sounding like galactic theological poetry, were a perfect candidate for inclusion in the church's Index of Prohibited Books, forbidden to all believers. Much later, the Vatican granted its approval for Catholics to read Teilhard's books. But to my mind, the church had every reason to be concerned about the author's philosophy, not because it was heretical or disrespectful to Catholic doctrine but because of the radicalism of its vast and liberating metaphysical vision.

Teilhard, who had died almost a decade before I read his work, was so far ahead of his time that even his most mechanical observations on biology and evolution read like flights of rarefied mysticism. He invented phrases such as the alpha point and the omega point, for the beginning and end of human evolution as it moved inexorably back to the Creator and the Cosmic Christ, for the process of spiritualizing the material universe.

He theorized about a noosphere, a "human layer" of the planet where collective human awareness exists and interacts endlessly with itself. Communications satellites and the Internet were still half a century in the future when Teilhard wrote about

an invisible layer of human consciousness surrounding Earth.
Today, concepts such as the big bang and the big crunch—
Teilhard's alpha and omega points—have entered mainstream
popular thinking and the noosphere, by any other name, is
something everyone accepts as a present reality.

Reading *The Phenomenon of Man*, I began to understand
that there was much more to spirituality than the religion to
which I had given myself with such conviction and devotion.
The sweeping panorama of intergalactic space and the drama
of human evolution through time arose in my imagination and
overwhelmed the rule-bound prison to which I consigned my
spiritual longings. Stimulated by Teilhard's vision, I yearned for
the freedom to create my own spiritual ideas and feelings.

I continued to contemplate my dilemma of how to be loyal
to my religion and at the same time be true to my spiritual aspirations. As I did so, I started to see that I would have to make a
final decision on the basis of what was working for me in my life
and what was not. Whenever I entertained the idea of living forever within the rule-bound structure of my religion, I felt sad
and dull. I also noticed I was sick more often with colds, flus,
aches, and pains. More than that, I sensed a kind of background
noise of melancholy in my life. I knew I was out of alignment,
not living according to the guidance of my conscience. By con-
trast, whenever I envisioned a life of spiritual seeking without
constraints I felt more alive, joyful, and healthy. The prospect
of seeking spiritual connection on my own thrilled me.

Grace set in motion a series of inner events that helped me
take action. I needed to bid good-bye to the religious structure
that nourished me in childhood but was increasingly irrelevant,

even obstructive, to me as an adult. Once I recognized my higher responsibility to myself, I turned away and did not look back. The moment I did, grace seemed to sweep in again to take me on an undreamed of spiritual adventure.

Joseph Campbell, the great scholar of world mythologies, said, "The hero takes up the challenge that is offered, and immediately the gods rush to his side to help." Once you decide to answer the call to create your own spiritual life outside religion, the road opens to a new and more meaningful connection to your spiritual Source.

You are never alone in your search. If you are a sincere spiritual seeker, the whole world of spirit is available to you. Books come, people come, special peak experiences come—grace comes. Making the decision to forge a personal spiritual life stirs everything into action, and you find yourself venturing bravely out.

PART TWO

seeking

CHAPTER THREE

sacred skeptic

If you would be a real seeker after truth, it is necessary that at least once in your life you doubt, as far as possible, all things.
—RENÉ DESCARTES, *DISCOURS DE LA MÉTHODE*

MY HAND QUIVERED as I prepared to open the envelope. The documents had arrived in the mail at my new address two days earlier, but I waited until now, with my mind clear and my courage plucked up, to open the large white envelope with regal Vatican postal stamps in the upper right corner and the crest of the Holy See in the upper left. From other brothers who had left the order, I had heard about the declaration of dispensation and the impact it was likely to have on me.

By that time, six months after informing my religious superiors that I wanted to petition a release from my vows, I was living back "in the world," in a small rented apartment a thousand miles from my monastery. I lingered there in a kind of suspended animation. Although I had left monastic life, until an official dispensation arrived I was still living under the obligations of my vows of poverty, chastity, and obedience.

As you can imagine, it was a peculiar time for me. I had left my community, which is all I had known for eight years, and was living by myself. I felt uprooted, dislocated, and utterly alone. In addition to leaving my religious order and my solemn vows, I had also given up my religion. In my mind at the time, the two were the same. I could not continue in conscience practicing my religion because my misgivings about it were what led me to renounce my monastic calling.

"Insofar as we are able . . ." the letter began. The words sent a chill through me. As I explained earlier, I had made my perpetual vows directly to God, not to the Catholic Church or my religious order. Here was the church saying that, as far as it was concerned, I had no further obligation to live the vows. But the implication was that unfinished business remained between God and me over the sacred promises. I did not know it at the time, but it would take years for me to come to terms with the first line of my formal dispensation.

The document, emblazoned with the impressive papal coat of arms, marked the end of one phase of my spiritual journey and the beginning of another. Slowly, I would pick up the pieces of my life and start the process of trying to build a personal spirituality on the ashes of my experience in monasticism—and in religion. I had known since I was a child that I had a calling to seek my creative Source. Now, with a painful but rich and powerful spiritual experience behind me, I was about to continue my search.

{ .. .. }

I believe we are all called to be spiritual seekers. In the human school, this is the one required course; it is not an elective.

You must have known this for a long time. Even as a child, you probably felt the pull to explore the spheres of life beyond what you could see and touch. As you matured into your teen years, you might have felt even more of a tug toward spiritual matters. In our teens, many of us experience a tremendous spiritual spike in the form of idealism and unconditional generosity. We become interested and curious about the big world out there and try to come up with some way of serving it. During this important time, many young people sign up for the military, the Peace Corps, or some other service or humanitarian venture. I entered a monastery.

Later, in early adulthood, you may hear the call to seek spirit once again. Usually, during our peak career years, the call is more difficult to hear. We are busy building our lives and may have less time for reflection. But even then, the awareness of ourselves as spiritual seekers and the yearning to explore that special realm of life stays with us. It often becomes more urgent as the years pass. Psychologist Carl Jung wrote, "Among all my patients in the second half of life, there has not been one whose problem in the last resort was not that of finding a religious [for which he meant "spiritual"] outlook on life."

The nineteenth-century philosopher Søren Kierkegaard said that we come into this world with sealed orders and spend the

Sacred Skeptic

rest of our lives learning what they say about why we are here. When we arrive on the planet, we immediately begin the return journey to our spiritual home base, collecting as much self-knowledge as we can along the way, following a unique roadmap of our own making. We are born seekers.

Vocation is a word ordinarily used to describe a divine call to the religious life or the priesthood. But we all have a vocation, a divine calling, to be spiritual seekers. Seeking is so much a part of the human experience that we do not even question it. We humans are forever in quest of new information and understanding, whether in the macro world of galaxies or the micro world of quarks. Spiritually, to look at the archeological and anthropological evidence, we have been seekers for as long as we have been human.

The Seeker is an archetype. Much has been written recently about archetypes; Jung was the first modern thinker to develop the concept. He visualized all of remembered human experience as accumulating in a giant storehouse, the collective unconscious. From it emerge characters and situations that everyone recognizes.

Archetypes are prototypes and perfect models, symbols that represent universal concepts, personality types, and human activities. The Hero, for instance, is an identifiable archetype in all of human experience. The Hero goes out on a quest to slay the dragon and bring home the trophy—an illustration in archetypal terms of the yearning in all of us to go out into the world, be successful at something, and return with proof that we have done the deed. On a deeper level, the Hero's quest is a metaphorical inner quest to overcome an obstacle or obtain self-knowledge, and to come home with the prize of new knowledge or a new spiritual awakening.

Archetypes are more familiar to us than we think. When we go to see a popular movie, we are watching archetypes in action. Movie actors become "stars" (beautiful, bright, remote, timeless) by connecting us with archetypal personalities in the collective unconscious. The Matinee Idol, with his clean-cut good looks and athletic physical abilities, is an archetype. The Ingénue, a young woman of charm, grace, beauty, and a bit of naiveté, is the Matinee Idol's feminine counterpart. These archetypal roles are filled by actors all through our popular entertainment history, with one being replaced by another as the "real people" age into other kinds of archetypes: in this case, the Matinee Idol might become a Father or Boss archetype, the Ingénue a Mother or Wise Woman archetype.

Universal personality types exist as archetypes, and so do universal human situations. A typical archetypal situation is corruption of power, and the madness that accompanies the fall of a person or a group. Repeatedly, through real history and in our fiction, we see this universal circumstance working itself out, whether it wears the mask of Napoleon Bonaparte or Charles Foster Kane.

"All the most powerful ideas in history go back to archetypes," Jung wrote. "This is particularly true of religious ideas." One member of a tribe sacrificing his life to save the entire tribe is a common religious archetype, whether the sacrificial victim is Jesus or Quetzalcóatl, Osiris or Iphigenia. Another is the avenging God that metes out punishment to evildoers—Zeus with thunderbolts, Jehovah with floods, Allah with the armies of the enemy. Hell, as we saw in the last chapter, is a religious archetype, and so is Heaven.

Archetypes are within us, part of us. They are usually activated by outer events and inner responses to those events, at which times they step more to the fore and help guide our decisions, and ultimately our lives. If you are driving on a highway and a tire fails, you may notice your inner Magician taking over to help you out of your predicament. If you are going into a contract negotiation, you may feel the Warrior archetype rising up in you to meet the challenge.

The Seeker, which also goes by the names Wanderer, Explorer, Nomad, and Vagabond, motivates you to search for a spiritual path. It kindles within you a passion to search for wisdom and learn lessons on the basis of the facts you uncover. It takes you through many philosophies, ideologies, religious traditions, and cultural customs to discover spiritual truth. It does all this tirelessly, with dedicated single-mindedness.

Carol Pearson, in her groundbreaking work on archetypes, *Awakening the Heroes Within,* says the Seeker's quest is for a better life—in a spiritual sense, a better spiritual life or path. The Seeker is motivated by fear of conformity. It possesses the noble virtues of autonomy and ambition. The task of the Seeker is to be true to the deeper self.

This wonderful energy operates in all of us simply because we are human. Although it is with us and at our service all the time, we can call it forth to assist in our spiritual search. I did not know about archetypes at the time I left monastic life, but I made a conscious effort to engage that part of me I knew had always been there and summoned its energy to continue my spiritual quest. My Seeker stepped forward.

One way I connected with my Seeker energy was by adopting a skeptical mind-set. The greatest difficulty I experienced

with religion was its fundamental premise (take this secondhand
spiritual truth on faith). To begin my search for a personal spirituality outside religion, I naturally gravitated toward a prove-it-
to-me position. On the surface, it might have looked as if I
were being a rebel and acting out against my religious past.
But deeper down, I thought of it as a kind of sacred skepticism,
because questioning everything I had been taught was really
essential if I were going to shape my own spiritual path.

"Authority has every reason to fear the skeptic," says psychoanalyst Robert Lindner, "for authority can rarely survive in the
face of doubt." Skepticism is an attitude of doubt or disposition
to incredulity. Sacred skepticism is this attitude applied to so-
called religious truth. It wants to find the underlying cause of
things by asking the hardest questions: Wait just a minute; is this
true? How do you know it is true? What evidence do you have
that it is true? What are your proofs? Is what you are telling me
true always and in every circumstance?

For instance, someone says an antique gold coin is hidden
under a large rock near your home. You would want to know if
the statement is true before going off to try to find the rock and
the coin. Who said it is true? How does that person know? What
evidence do you have that there is an antique gold coin there, or
even that there is a large rock?

In the traditional religions, we are told that if we believe
the gold coin is under a rock, we are acceptable in the eyes of
God ("blessed are those who believe"). The sacred skeptic
questions everything about the hidden treasure in an effort
to actually seek out the rock and possess the coin. You cannot
truly own something, in other words, unless you have an experience of it.

Sacred Skeptic

To build a unique spiritual way for yourself, you need to ask difficult questions of people and institutions that purport to know spiritual truth. With organized religion, the dead end is always the point at which you are told "There is no proof for this, nor can there ever be; you must believe it on faith." This is not an adequate response for the spiritual seeker, who is asking the eternal questions. Too much is at stake to take someone else's word for truth without evidence. In the case of traditional organized religions, the believer (an apt word in this context) is asked to take the word of someone from the long distant past who offered no proofs of truth then and certainly cannot offer any now.

The Seeker is on a sacred quest for spiritual truth. When you are starting to build your own spiritual truth outside religion, the first challenge you are likely to encounter is that all the spiritual truth you need to know has already been revealed by God, and you can find it between the covers of a big book. You do not have to search for anything because learned men (always men) down through the ages have done it for you. They were God's special instruments; therefore everything they wrote comes straight from God, who is telling you what to do and what not to do.

The world's great religions are based on beliefs clustered around sacred books. The Torah, the Bible, and the Qur'an are the sometimes-overlapping or cross-referencing scriptures of the three monotheistic religions, whose ranks make up 53 percent of the world's population. They contain both the history of the believers and the content of their beliefs. The holy books of all the religions, and their support texts, were written over long stretches of time by many authors in a variety of styles and from an assortment of worldviews. The Old Testament of the Bible took around fifteen hundred years to complete.

Colossal disputes raged among many highly schooled people through several eras of history regarding which writings should be included in the final versions of the books. Some writings won and some lost, often on political, social, or other nontheological grounds. The Bible, as it has come down to us, appears to have been compiled from many sources by one man, Bishop Eusebius of Caesarea. In 325, the emperor Constantine put an end to the heated conflict of competing theologians and princes by simply ordering Eusebius to deliver fifty copies of a completed bible to him. The bishop complied and by the end of the century his compilation was upheld as the canon. Even after the sacred texts of the various religions were codified, they were translated into and out of dozens of languages, introducing a considerable assortment of meanings to central concepts.

I am thinking primarily of the Bible, the sacred text most familiar to me. But the same can be said about the Qur'an and Eastern scriptures such as the most important texts of Hinduism, the Four Vedas, and the *Bhagavad-Gita,* which influenced many other Eastern religions. Each is a compilation of writings pieced together like a patchwork quilt to form a canon, or body of spiritual beliefs.

All these books claim divine origin. The religions that have the Bible as their foundational sacred text say it is divinely inspired; that is, although it may have been written by many authors over many years, every word in it actually was written by God, working through the human authors. Thus we have "the word of God," the basis of belief directly from the Source. The Qur'an is the revealed text that Muslims believe was dictated by the angel Gabriel to Muhammad, the greatest and final of the prophets of God.

But of course, the Bible and all the sacred texts of the world's many religions were written by people like you and me. The sacred skeptic remembers that we invented both God and the holy books that contain the presumed word of God. They can be called revelations from on high, but they remain quite human in origin—and the God at the center of them acts in suspiciously human ways. The God of the Bible did not make us in his image; we made him in our image.

This is not to say that sacred texts are of no use in inspiring you on your personal spiritual path. However, substituting this received and codified wisdom—someone's path, perhaps, but not yours—for the opportunity of direct contact with your Source certainly would limit the parameters of your spiritual search. In other words, owning the Bible as the totality of your own path is a little like saying that you can learn all you need to know about American culture from reading one novel by Ernest Hemingway.

The Seeker, armed with a keen skepticism, approaches sacred texts as fascinating spiritual writing but carefully weighs their recommendations for and proscriptions against human behavior. You may find some of what appears in the Bible is sensible, such as loving your neighbor, a directive that appears in one form or another in virtually all the sacred texts. But you may also find the encouragement to kill people who do not believe what you believe (Luke 19:27) at least questionable.

For the Seeker, the problem with all holy books is that they end debate so abruptly. If you pursue the question of evil, for instance (Is evil a real thing? Does it exist in the world as something apart from people? Why do some people seem to be evil?), you discover answers in all the holy books, but they are not your answers, and so you may find that they have little meaning for you. Unless you ponder the question of evil on your own, as many seekers have done for years, you will not come to an understanding of the matter. You will never know how it fits into your personal spiritual picture.

Creeds and dogmas operate in the same way. Sometimes they are inherent in the holy scriptures of the religions, but they are often extrapolated from the books and come down to us encrusted with tradition and custom. These collections of doctrines, the body of belief, were accumulated over centuries, just like the sacred books. Some of the creeds are tremendous testaments of faith, and referring to them when building a personal approach to spirituality can be enlightening. But the Seeker is on the lookout for warmed-over wisdom and the intrinsically nonsensical.

For instance, it is a doctrine of the Catholic religion that Mary, the mother of Jesus, was "assumed bodily into heaven" at her death. To believe that (and you must, if you are a Catholic), you would have to believe in the first place that there is a heaven above the clouds to which Mary's body could be assumed or taken up. This is not a part of religious folklore from the distant past, and therefore excusable as inherited dogmatic baggage dragged into today's world; it is one of the most recent of Catholic dogmas. Pope Pius XII declared it infallible in 1950.

Later, I suggest ways in which you can take nuggets of spiritual truth from some of the religious doctrines and decide whether you want to make them your own spiritual truth. The dogma of the literal Assumption of Mary seems like a stretch, but honoring the Divine Feminine archetype in ourselves and in the world certainly is one of the elements in a sound personal spirituality.

Some religions, especially the more progressive Protestant sects, say they are open to spiritual seeking within their doctrinal boundaries. Blind faith is not required to belong to these churches, according to them, and in fact it is discouraged. But I remain skeptical, like a good Seeker. If someone is a member of a church, which is to say an organization that espouses a body of beliefs, the person has found a spiritual path. Authentic seeking by definition needs to be done outside the walls of an established religious faith.

{ .. .. }

The Seeker questions everything. A skeptical viewpoint is the best resource for starting to create a personal spiritual way of life. You may find this radical approach difficult to contemplate, and even more difficult to activate in yourself. You may also consider it somehow disloyal or dishonest. Would-be seekers, shrinking from this important spiritual task, may take cover in the paradoxical notion that by seeking they are being sinful—as if sin were not a fabricated idea and part of the very system they are fleeing for spiritual freedom.

Fortunately, we have numerous role models for seeking at this important time in history when we are leaving the limitations of religion and beginning to explore spirituality in different ways. Seekers have always been with us, inspiring us to go out on our own and look for spiritual truth. Recently, in response to the yearning that so many of us are feeling to chart our own spiritual course outside the traditional routes, many writers and thinkers have been appearing to help us in our search.

You are already aware of these seekers. They range from scientists such as the late Carl Sagan to medical doctors such as Deepak Chopra, Larry Dossey, and Andrew Weil, from social commentator Marianne Williamson and psychologist Wayne Dyer to theologian Matthew Fox and spiritual teacher Ram Dass.

Over the years of my own seeking, I have admired these charismatic seekers and their work; occasionally I have had the opportunity to meet some of them and discuss their vision. One of the most impressive was Shirley MacLaine. The first time I met her, she and I were out in the country near Santa Fe attending a private workshop on the subject of faith healing. A Philippine healer was demonstrating how he dug his fingers directly into the stomach of a sick person to pull out cancerous tumors and other harmful tissue. Later that day, we would receive one of these "faith operations" from him.

During a break, I sat under a tree with MacLaine and we spoke about the process of spiritual seeking. Although she had been an internationally famous movie star for more than thirty years, she was just beginning to come into public awareness as a spiritual seeker. Her first book, *Out on a Limb*, about her explorations of out-of-body travel and reincarnation, had been published a few months earlier.

At that time, it seemed incongruous, to say the least, that a movie star would be writing about spiritual seeking. She was risking the credibility of her long and extraordinary career by revealing her interest in nonmainstream spiritual thinking and encouraging others to undertake their own spiritual investigation. But when I asked her about it, she reminded me that part of being a spiritual seeker is not being ashamed or afraid to tell what you are discovering. Besides, so much is at stake now.

"I like to think of it this way," she said, sipping on the allowed green tea during our strict fast, "God may have made me famous so he could use me to get new spiritual information to large numbers of people quickly."

In her spiritual search, MacLaine was evolving a truth for herself that she could share with millions of others. After her innumerable trips back in time to past lives, her visits to the sacred sites of Machu Picchu, Stonehenge, and Santiago de Compostela, and her many autobiographical writings, she was able to report: "Maybe the tragedy of the human race was that we had forgotten that we are each divine."

These seekers and many others like them are not suggesting that you and I follow their path. In fact, the whole point of being a Seeker is to pursue one's own way and find one's own spiritual truth. However, they are splendid exemplars, reminding us that seeking is what we are here to do—and that sacred skepticism, which they encourage, can help us create our own special path.

{ .. .. }

After I left monastic life and my Catholic religion, I spent several years wandering on a directionless inner journey. I experimented with psychotropic substances such as magic mushrooms, peyote, and LSD but did not find them to be helpful in my spiritual growth. Drugs are often touted as a shortcut to the Source, but there really are no shortcuts. My experience has been that drugs do not take you to the face of God. They only delay the process of high spiritual awareness.

I tried a number of therapies as well, including an anger-based method that had me punching pillows for hours on end as a facilitator shouted at me. That was interesting and exhausting but did not seem to lead anywhere. Individual talk counseling with a sympathetic former nun did little at the time to advance my search.

For a long time, I attended all the latest workshops and lectures of a spiritual nature. I learned about Findhorn in Scotland, where people were growing cabbages in the sand with spiritual energy and a spoonful of compost. I became familiar with esoteric astrology and the mysteries of the Tarot. I showed up at EST. I studied and comprehended most of what I read of the new quantum physics, which was bringing the physical universe ever closer to the spiritual vision I glimpsed reading Teilhard de Chardin.

I delved into the works of several contemporary gurus, including the great Swami Muktananda, and later his radiant successor, Gurumayi Chidvilasananda. As much as I was drawn to their wonderful philosophy of love and compassion, I encountered the same fundamental dilemma that had haunted my years in the Catholic religion: I was being asked to adopt someone else's spiritual truth. Moreover, the chants, homilies, meditation practices, and flowers-and-incense rituals were too reminiscent of the religious trappings from which I had so recently walked away.

Some of my wandering must have seemed rather pointless at the time, but now I understand that everything was preparation for the next step up in my spiritual awareness. From the perspective of the present, it appears the Seeker archetype was working powerfully in me and for me.

In addition to my inner search, I was trying to live a reasonably normal life. My vows, for all their undeniable spiritual substance, left me somewhat helpless in huge areas of life. The vow of poverty gave me a distorted sense of the value of money. Chastity rendered me naïve and inexperienced in relationships. Obedience undermined my personal power often making it difficult for me to make a good decision or any decision at all.

In spite of these handicaps, I managed. In monastic life, I was trained as an educator. Soon I was teaching again, making new friends, and building a new kind of life. My spiritual search continued and continues to this day, but gradually it came into balance with all the other parts of my life that needed attention. Much later I would understand that living an ordinary, day-to-day life with integrity and impeccability is most of what it means to be "spiritual."

Seeking wisdom and truth is one of our essential human pursuits. We are truly human when we are looking for the next higher place in self-awareness. However, there is a shadow side to the Seeker archetype. The Seeker cannot stop seeking. Now and then during that feverish period, I felt I might have been going too fast. I wondered whether I should be giving more attention to each of my spiritual investigations before dropping them to take up the next one in line.

If we are always seeking and never finding, we may be in danger of sinking into a dark and lonely place. Shadow Seekers are lost souls, constantly out on the road looking for home but never coming to rest in a sense of belonging with community. I used to run into them at workshops. These determined Seekers were so absorbed in their search that they seemed to forget their original goal of spiritual enlightenment. This was a pity, I thought, because compulsive seeking was preventing them from receiving the information they so ardently desired. They would take up with one spiritual teacher, but even before they had heard the entire instruction the shadow of the Seeker archetype would kick in and they would be off to another teacher, only to repeat the same circular sequence of events.

Seekers who fall into the shadow are never content, never fulfilled, never connected. A song by U2 describes their experience: "I still haven't found what I'm looking for."

You may have met people like this. They travel a great deal but never seem to be comfortable in any one place. They hop around among careers. They move from apartment to apartment, house to house, without achieving what they really want and need, a true home. They do not finish things but instead run on to the next possibility, the next opportunity for seeking. Victims of addiction are invariably driven by the shadow of the Seeker archetype.

I remember a caution from one of my teachers, the American mystic Joel Goldsmith. Later I will have much to say about Joel, but here he is on the subject of the shadow Seeker: "By all means, go and seek. But once you have found your spiritual truth, it is time for you to stop your search and begin to live that truth." The shadow Seeker, by obsessive seeking, is always denied the peace of mind that living spiritual truth brings.

If you have found yourself caught up in excessive seeking, whether inside or outside organized religion, you are in good company. Siddhartha Gautama spent many years wandering through India, fasting, feasting, and listening to teachers, before he came to rest beneath the Bodhi tree, understood that he was one with all there is, and became the Buddha.

The challenge for the spiritual seeker is to come to the end of searching. If you have done your inner homework, you will find that the end comes about quite naturally. Something clicks within you. There is an "ah-ha." Seeking is never truly over, but the urgency of the exploration loses its energy as you relax into the tranquil place of living your spiritual truth.

When you go forth from the comforts of religion, with its "revealed" truths, doctrines, and formulas that tend to lull the soul to sleep, taking on the attitude of a professional seeker will keep you awake and open to life-changing spiritual insights. After I embraced a sacred skepticism and began to question the entire spiritual worldview of my childhood, doors opened. I began to see some of the thrilling, infinite possibilities of living in connection with my Source.

Wonderful work awaited me. The more I saw myself as a professional seeker, the more I found I needed to tear down some dilapidated inner structures so that new ones could be built. In that amazing process towers of useless beliefs would topple and walls of false values would crumble.

CHAPTER FOUR

beliefs

A belief is not merely an idea the mind possesses; it is an idea that possesses the mind.
—ROBERT BOLTON

WHAT IF THERE were no such thing as God? What if all the stories about a Divine Being we have been receiving from other people for thousands of years were elaborate fantasies? What if we woke up tomorrow morning to discover that humans of the past made up God to solve mysteries in the world they could not explain, and we have been living with that figment of the human imagination ever since?

What if our species has been laboring under an illusion since around 2000 B.C., thinking there is a Supreme Being somewhere who is like us, created us, maintains us in existence, and will judge us after we die? What if there never were a God and he never spoke to people or left a record of his words in big books of sacred scriptures? What if the holy books of the world religions were not written or even "inspired" by a grand divine personage, but were made up by ordinary people like you and me?

All of this may seem like blasphemy for those still tied to a traditional religion. Even if not, these questions can leave a bitter taste in the mouth. Our whole culture rests on Christian principles. To suggest openly that the God of the monotheistic religions, including Islam, does not exist is considered disrespectful at the least, if not downright immoral in some quarters, deserving of punishment. In our country, with its strong Christian identification (*God* is on our money, in our loyalty pledge, in our courts—we swear to God on a Bible to tell the truth), you would be extremely careful about saying in public that God is a pure fiction. Atheistic activists often come to a bad end. Go into a fundamentalist Islamic culture and suggest that Allah may be as imaginary as a unicorn, and you will find yourself running for cover.

Yet the true spiritual seeker must be willing to entertain these questions, and many more, before building a strong and meaningful personal spirituality. If you leave old spiritual ideas standing in the process of moving away from religion, there will be no room for brilliant and expansive new ideas.

{ .. .. }

Our beliefs define us. Everything we think and do is filtered through our beliefs. They frame our inner pictures of ourselves and other people, and the rest of the world. If you believe the world is a dangerous place, every interaction you have with people carries underlying themes of suspicion, fear, and mistrust. You have your guard up constantly, expecting something awful to happen at any moment. Similarly, if you believe that the world is a safe place, you live your life with confidence, wonder, and joy, meeting every situation with a smile on your face and a spring in your step.

Think of your belief system as a window through which you see this breathtakingly beautiful world. Contaminated beliefs—junk thinking inherited from other people, cultural propaganda promoting ideologies and lifestyles, worldviews based on advertising products for consumption, superstitions of all kinds, outright misinformation, unquestioned truths, ignorant conjectures, free-floating fears, and the rest—are like prison bars on your window. Every time you look out you see the world through the distortion of those tainted filters.

You build your individual identity as well on the basis of what you see through the prison bars of accumulated misinformation. These filtered views become your core beliefs about yourself. Common negative core beliefs are "I'm not good enough," "I'm a failure," "I'm not important," "I'm not worthy of love," "I don't deserve to be prosperous," and "I'm powerless." Imagine trying to realize your highest potential if you are convinced by your beliefs that you never can.

Core beliefs work most effectively when we are not aware of them. The less conscious we are of their nature and how they are working in us, the better chance they have to sabotage everything we turn our hand to.

One more thing about beliefs is that when you believe a certain thing you are bound to its consequences. If you do not believe it, you are free of its rules of retribution or retaliation. Say you truly believe people are inherently bad. You encounter a new acquaintance, with the intention of forging a friendship. However, since you view people as being bad, the person is sure to eventually treat you poorly, betray you, and abandon you. Responding to your inner image, the person really has no other choice. If you continue holding that toxic belief, you attract into your circle only those who will sooner or later do their dirty work and leave.

Spiritual core beliefs operate in the same way. If you believe you come into this world as a damaged, sinful creature unworthy of divine love, you will live in dread of impending punishment, forever striving for a connection to your creative Source. This connection must forever elude you. By the same example, if you believe you are fundamentally sinful but can by "saved" by some kind of religious intervention, you will get yourself to a religion that promises redemption. Then you will stay there even if your heart tells you that many of the other religious messages you bought into are absurd.

How do you know what your core beliefs are? This can be slippery territory, because beliefs have such a hold on us. It can be difficult trying to glimpse the real world from the prison window. However, there are ways to identify your beliefs. You can find books that offer core belief inventories. The Internet lists dozens of them. Among other approaches, you may want to look into the work of Byron Katie (www.thework.com), who has her students unearth core beliefs by asking four elementary questions:

1. Is it true?
2. Can you absolutely know that it is true?
3. How do you react when you think that thought?
4. Who would you be without the thought?

Any of these probes is helpful, but in the end you return to your initial intuition on the questions that color your personal spiritual vision: Is there a God? Only one God? Does prayer have any meaning? Is there sin, heaven, hell, the devil? You are the best judge and highest authority on these essential issues.

{ .. .. }

In the previous chapter we looked at archetypes, particularly the Seeker. Many archetypal energies having their own unique character reside within us. These archetypes are collective human personae or masks. When we decide to put one on we empower ourselves with the energy of that mask. You know how this works if you have donned a disguise for a Halloween party and found that it could change your entire personality. Put on a horrific devil mask and look in the mirror, and a surge of feelings come up in you. Getting in touch with inner archetypes works in the same way.

The Seeker pushes you out on the road and encourages you to probe and investigate the realm of spirituality. While that energy is running in you, assuming you are searching widely and deeply enough, another archetype begins to emerge. The Destroyer may sound like something terrible, but actually it is an exceptionally positive energy. When you connect with your inner Destroyer, you are able to tear down the old attitudes and concepts that threaten to block your progress.

Think of it this way. In an otherwise exciting, vibrant urban center, there is a city block of decaying, abandoned buildings. The area has been neglected for years. People throw trash and garbage there. Rats run around at night among the rusting tin cans and broken glass. Now, you are the town's top architect.

You have been commissioned to build a cluster of glimmering new buildings on that spot, your dream project, but you cannot proceed with construction until the land is cleared.

This is when Destroyer energy takes over. Without it, you would not be able to go ahead with your plans for the future. The Destroyer is a dismantler, a wrecker of stale and unusable ideas and inner pictures. In Hindu tradition, it is Shiva, Destroyer of the World. In Persian mythology, it is Angra Mainya, the God of Darkness, the Eternal Destroyer. The Celtic tradition's Destroyer is the great goddess Cailech. For the ancient Hebrews, Yahweh was a Destroyer who brought down cities and caused worldwide natural disasters, such as the flood from which Noah was spared. Among the Bible's many other Destroyers are the Four Horsemen of the Apocalypse: War, Pestilence, Famine, and Death.

In Roman mythology, Pluto is the ultimate Destroyer, King of the Underworld. Thus in astrology the planet Pluto, which rules the sign of Scorpio, symbolizes death to everything in our lives that is old and unworkable. Popular culture is awash in the Destroyer archetype—particularly blockbuster movies, with their thundering explosions and apocalyptic visions.

You are aware of how the Destroyer archetype has operated in your life up to now. We all experience the Destroyer at life's transition points. As teenagers, we dismantle our childhood relationships with our parents and siblings. As adults, we tear down and leave behind the habits and liaisons of our naïve teen years. Every new life passage calls forth the Destroyer to help us make a space for the next definition of ourselves.

If the notion of carrying around a Destroyer inside you makes you nervous, like toting a bomb that might detonate itself at any second, remember that even though all the archetypes are always in us only the ones we consciously call forth are truly active. If you have reached a bottleneck in some area of your life, you may want to bring up your Destroyer to blow up the blockage. Until then, it is resting.

The Destroyer tears down and rips up, only to empty out an area where something better can be constructed. In myths and esoteric traditions, the Destroyer is often coupled with the Creator archetype, to convey the concept of razing something specifically to rebuild in its place. If the Destroyer begins to dismantle structures just for the thrill of it, the archetype moves into the shadow side.

Destroyer energy applied to our spiritual seeking offers a powerful opportunity to clear away the debris of other people's spiritual ideas, attitudes, and judgments that over the years, regardless of their validity, you have made your own. During the process of seeking, you can call it in to bulldoze away the decaying structures of core spiritual beliefs borrowed from the past, handed down, patched up, left in the sun, and otherwise rendered useless to you in creating your personal spiritual vision.

The Destroyer in you works hand-in-hand with the Seeker. First the Seeker surveys the scene to get the lay of the land. This keen investigative force digs things up like a plow turning up the earth to prepare a field for planting. Once the Seeker has done its job of laying bare everything you need to appraise, the Destroyer can come in to clear away all the nonessentials. In spiritual terms, the Seeker shows you what core beliefs are driving your thoughts and feelings, and the Destroyer knocks down the ones that do not fit into your head and heart anymore.

My experience with the destruction process has been curious, and I pass this on as a caution for you. When I left monastic life and began looking outside religion for a strong personal connection to my Source, I felt a strange reticence setting in. A small, rebellious part of me wanted to barge into my belief system and start leveling everything in sight, but mostly I shied away from doing anything at all about what I believed. I had owned my beliefs for a long time; they were my companions, in a way, my intellectual and emotional support structure. When new spiritual ideas came flooding in, my beliefs, forged over years, dealt with them. I measured them against what I believed was the truth, discarding them if they did not match up. I wanted to be loyal to my old beliefs.

Something else held me back from looking squarely at my beliefs with the goal of throwing at least some of them out. The religious beliefs I was about to pull out had long roots. They came from my parents and from their parents before them. They were nurtured through my childhood with loving attention and the best of intentions. Throwing out my beliefs was in a peculiar way throwing out my family history and legacy as well.

I would have gotten permanently stuck at that stage if I had not confronted it head on. Difficult as it was, I discussed with my parents what I was contemplating doing. I had already given up the practice of my religion. Now I wanted to go further and explore a world without any religious beliefs, not even the existence of God. At first, they expressed their discomfort with what I was doing. There was even a hint that on some level I was betraying them. However, when they understood the process I had begun toward developing a spirituality of my own, they gave me their support.

Because our beliefs have been with us for so long, we tend
to be quite devoted to them. Embarking on the process of tearing
them down, we are likely to feel restrained in the beginning. Looking back now, I see that my reticence probably was a delay tactic.
I encourage you to look clearly and fearlessly at what you truly
believe about spirituality—what you inherited from your parents,
your grandparents, your teachers, your family and friends, your
coworkers. Sorting through the baggage of ideas, notions, concepts,
dogmas, inner pictures, and opinions can be tremendously revealing. I remember throwing up my hands at one point during my
own process. If this idea had come from my parish priest, that
concept from my grandparents, and those prejudices from my
second-grade teacher, then who or what was the real me?

{ .. .. }

My spiritual seeking led me to many areas of the mind and heart,
as well as to many geographical areas. After leaving my monastery
in Indiana, I completed postgraduate studies in cinema history in
Texas and then took a position in Washington, D.C., with the
American Film Institute. After that, I moved to Los Angeles to
work in the movie industry. If it sounds incompatible to you that
a former monk would be writing and editing movie scripts for
United Artists in Hollywood, I can say it was just as much of a
surprise to me. I felt drawn to explore my creative side, and in
the back of my mind I probably imagined I could help bring a
spiritual dimension to popular entertainment.

After two years, however, I wanted to live in a smaller community, one more conducive to my spiritual search. I moved to
Santa Fe, New Mexico, where I found a group of like-minded
people. At first, I thought Santa Fe might be just another stop on

Beliefs

my investigative journey of the spirit. But the town, in the midst
of a spiritual ferment at that time and full of seekers like me,
was so supportive of my spiritual aspirations that I ended up
living there for the next twenty-four years.

The adage "When the student is ready, the teacher will
appear" was certainly true in my case. Shortly after I arrived
in Santa Fe, a brilliant teacher appeared. Hazel Larsen Archer,
a soft-spoken woman with short-cropped cotton-white hair,
was teaching a class called "An Investigation of Perception" to
artists. I eagerly began to study with her.

Hazel had been a member of the community at the fabled
Black Mountain College in North Carolina in the 1940s. Black
Mountain, founded in 1933, was the first American experimen-
tal college with democratic self-rule. Students and teachers lived
communally and studied in informal classes that fostered a
strong interdisciplinary approach to the liberal and fine arts.
By the time it closed its doors in the mid-1950s, its model had
been copied by scores of other institutions of higher learning.

Hazel Archer associated with many remarkable people at
Black Mountain: painters Josef Albers, Willem de Kooning,
Robert Rauschenberg, and Robert Motherwell; writers Alfred
Kazin and Charles Olson; composer John Cage; and dancer and
choreographer Merce Cunningham. The man who influenced
her most was architect Buckminster Fuller, who constructed his
first geodesic dome on the college campus. She credited Fuller
with helping her see the whole world differently by introducing
her to the perfection of what he called "nature's geometry."

Hazel herself was a photographer, but her keen observations
of life were not confined to the viewfinder. She was interested in

perception—how people see things, and how they are motivated by and act out of their unique vision of themselves and their environment. She said we are all born free of anyone else's definitions of the world but slowly acquire "sticks" of information, most of them false if well intentioned, until, like pack animals, we are carrying around huge bundles of these sticks. Entering adulthood, we are so heavily weighed down with bundles of fictitious, worthless, and dangerously erroneous information that we can barely stand up mentally, emotionally, and spiritually, and sometimes even physically. The process of seeing clearly, she discovered, can change a person's life, often instantaneously.

For Hazel, core beliefs about God are part of our perceptual bundle. Just as in inspired art, the process of seeking a spiritual path was inextricably tied to seeing without judging. "Observe your process," she would say repeatedly. "Watch what you think, what you say, how you say it. Do not judge; only watch, observe." In this way, she told us, we could begin to let go of the bundles we were hauling around and be open to true transformation: "When you learn to watch without judgment and opinion, what you had not recognized previously begins to surface as some kind of surprise—and you come to new awareness of yourself."

If that sounds like a mighty task, you are correct. For the next two years, I practiced simply watching the process without evaluation. I wish I could report that I felt the self-defeating bundles of other people's misperceptions melt off me, but it did not work that way. Gradually, though, I began to see people and situations in my life differently. Nowhere was this more apparent than in my spiritual strivings.

Beliefs

{ .. .. }

One day, as I was mindlessly puttering around in my kitchen, the words "Our Father" popped up in my head and would not go away. Later, I sat down and began to think about the central prayer of my Christian upbringing. I tried not to judge or evaluate, just to observe, as Hazel had taught me. Without doing or thinking anything, I felt my heart open. A thrill ran through my body like an electrical current. In the time it would have taken to snap my fingers, a complete picture of what we call the Lord's Prayer presented itself to me in total knowing. I was ambushed—blissfully so—by the miracle of perception.

What moved me so much was a sobering flash of understanding. The principal prayer of Western civilization, instead of helping to establish the bond we are all seeking between our Source and us, actually has been keeping us utterly and eternally apart. The Lord's Prayer is not about spiritual union with God; it is a heartbreaking hymn of separation.

> Our Father who art in heaven, hallowed be thy name.
> Thy kingdom come. Thy will be done in earth as it is in
> heaven. Give us this day our daily bread. And forgive us
> our trespasses, as we forgive them that trespass against
> us. And lead us not into temptation. But deliver us from
> evil. Amen [*Book of Common Prayer*, 1559].

The Lord's Prayer is probably the most famous prayer in the whole world. The title refers specifically to the prayer that Jesus, "the Lord," taught his followers, responding to their request in two of the four gospels: "Lord, teach us how to pray." But *Lord* also suggests God himself, so that it becomes a prayer to God, our Lord, as well.

The first six words tell the entire story of unbridgeable separation. There is a God, and he is in heaven. He is not here with us or in us. On the contrary, he is far off in a place called heaven, which in the cosmology of the Middle Ages is high above us, in the sky beyond the clouds, beyond the stars. The medieval worldview, with earth below and heaven above, persists in the religious imagination, no matter what the calculations of science and our own eyes peering through the Hubble Telescope tell us. Such has been the hold of the Lord's Prayer on the human psyche.

In the first half, we, the supplicants, are addressing God the King to be in his favor. We say who he is (Father), then where he is (in heaven), then how he is (hallowed or holy). We go on to say that we hope his dominion, which is now over heaven, will be extended to earth, where we are.

The God we invented around four thousand years ago has appeared in the human imagination wearing many masks. In the Old Testament of the Bible, which is the touchstone for the three great monotheistic religions, he is angry, terrifying, demanding, occasionally helpful, vengeful, annoyed, hard to please, sometimes merciful, usually merciless—and as volatile as a megalomaniac on a rampage. If you do not do exactly as he says, he will smite you and you will die.

In the New Testament, which only Christians regard as revealed spiritual truth, he is depicted as softer, but nonetheless in charge and judging. Jesus invariably addressed him as "Father," suggesting a warm parental connection. Early in the Christian era theologians went back and forth about God's personality often retreating into fanciful abstract worlds inhabited by unmoved movers, pure potencies, and holy trinities. During the Middle Ages, when feudalism was in flower, God's "Lord" aspect was emphasized and he was conceived as a super-monarch sitting on a throne.

The God-as-king idea has existed as a theme in our successive cultures for as long as we had human kings. We took that image literally for a long time. The ancient Egyptians took it so literally that when they buried their human kings they duplicated everything the person would need to be king (God) in the great beyond. They sent their god-king back to heaven in a real boat, propelled by real oarsmen, freshly put to death when the god-king was ready to start his return journey to the other world. Their tombs are virtual encyclopedias of the God-as-king cultural view.

For the ancient Romans, the idea of the royal divinity was so entrenched in consciousness that the emperors automatically became heavenly gods at the moment they ascended their earthly thrones. The strict traditional concept of god-king may have blurred somewhat with a few of the Roman emperors, whose human personalities were about as far from godlike as could be imagined. The Romans were always careful to keep the office separate from the person, however—a practice that allowed them to venerate a psychopath like Caligula, and also to have him assassinated.

Later on, long after kings had given up the pretense of being literally divine, they still were consecrated, "made sacred," as monarchs in the presence of God. Going to a cathedral to get your crown and scepter was the only acceptable practice in the

Middle Ages. In fact, the word cathedral comes from the Latin *cathedra,* meaning "throne"—specifically, the bishop's throne, the metaphor for God's ultimate majestic authority. Thus from the throne of God to the throne of the earthly king.

When Charlemagne was crowned Holy Roman Emperor at Saint Peter's Basilica in Rome on Christmas Day in 800, Pope Leo III himself placed the diadem on the king's head. The *Liber Pontificalis* (Book of the Popes) recorded the cry that was repeated three times before the tomb of Saint Peter: "To Charles, most pious Augustus, crowned by God . . . long life and victory!" For the occasion, Charlemagne is said to have worn a voluminous cape of dark purple, on which the heavenly constellations were embroidered in jewels. If there was any doubt about the connection between heavenly God and earthly king, Charlemagne pretty much dispelled it.

Much of what we were taught about God as children was formulated in Europe in the Middle Ages, when the Christian church held absolute political and moral dominance over the Western world. I would argue that this is still the case, of course. In this model, God is a king seated on a throne in a place called heaven surrounded by a court. The view has persisted in human consciousness for at least a thousand years, up to today.

Naturally, the god-king model is a metaphor, but one that carries enormous weight. The meaning behind it, regardless of how the symbol is framed, is that there is a God and he exists apart from us.

The first half of "The Lord's Prayer" defines God and sets up the gulf that exists between him and us. The second half is our supplication to that perfect, unreachable divinity. We ask God for four things, which, taken together, describe our essential nature: we need sustenance, forgiveness, not to be tempted, and deliverance from evil. To ask God for them requires that we believe we are powerless, we are sinful, we are weak, and we are helpless.

Our core beliefs define us. I understood, in the moment of insight in my kitchen, that every time I recited the Lord's Prayer I was reinforcing a host of negative spiritual core beliefs. I was saying that my Source was inaccessible and unapproachable, and that I am powerless, unworthy, and corrupt. If there is such a thing as spiritual low self-esteem, I had it, and so did everyone else seeking spiritual connection who innocently repeated "Our Father, who art in heaven . . ."

The strong message we get from the Lord's Prayer is that we are fundamentally flawed but there is a creator, somewhere far away from us, who is withholding from us all the basic things we need for our fulfillment. No wonder we are all walking around under our own little personal cloud of guilt. We declare that we are worthless, and to make things worse we have no hope of ever becoming less worthless. That is, if we keep praying the way we have been.

Let me make it clear that I am not suggesting the Lord's Prayer be stricken from the books and erased from the minds of billions of people. I am pointing out the core spiritual beliefs running behind the world's most well-known prayer. You can do the same with virtually any prayer or hymn you learned by rote as a child growing up within an organized religion, or simply in our Christian-dominated culture. All have core beliefs behind them; all have spiritual secrets to reveal.

When I told Hazel Archer about my new understanding of
the Lord's Prayer, she was pleased that the process of perception
seemed to be working in me. She also told me that her mentor
and friend, Buckminster Fuller, had contemplated the prayer
as well and come up with a poetic version of it that bridged
the gulf between God and us. Fuller's "Lord's Prayer" began
this way:

> Our God, who art in we even,
> Omni-experienced is your identity,
> the everywhere and everywhen evolving omnireality
> is your presence. . . .

{ .. .. }

As a sincere seeker navigating the ins and outs of a personal
spiritual path, you are bound to encounter, like surprise potholes
on the road, some of your past spiritual beliefs. Be aware that
standing in the shadows behind such familiar expressions of
worship as the Lord's Prayer, the Ten Commandments, Psalm 23
("The Lord is my shepherd . . ."), "Allahu Akbar" (God is Most
Great), and others are powerful messages about who you are,
and who or what your Source is in relation to you.

When these old beliefs come up, your first reaction may
be to sidestep the issues they raise. We tend to be loyal to our
beliefs, whether they promote or impede our personal growth.
But your spiritual seeking is best served by looking squarely
at familiar and treasured prayers, formulas, invocations, and
blessings. See them for what they are really saying—what *you*
are really saying—and decide whether you want to base your

Beliefs

personal spirituality on the core beliefs hidden in their sometimes beautifully crafted prose.

The Destroyer always tears down to build up. The purpose
of demolishing old, unhealthy spiritual core beliefs is to create
new, healthy ones in their place. As you come up against the
prayers of the past, consider substituting new beliefs for ones
that reinforce negative definitions of yourself and the center
of spirit, which is the end of your seeking.

After I saw what was behind the traditional Lord's Prayer,
I decided not to say it anymore, even in so-called neutral set-
tings. I created my own version of it, a prayer that has meaning
for me, because it emerged out of my personal spiritual search:

Thank you, Source of our lives, for already having given
us all we need for this fascinating journey in the flesh—
and thank you also for continuing to be here when we
have not fully grasped our fundamental connection to
you. May we always remember that unbreakable bond—
but if we forget, remind us, lest we begin to believe the
unthinkable: that we are somehow separated from you.
Amen.

CHAPTER FIVE

discernment

We shall not cease from exploration,
and the end of all our exploring will be to arrive where we started,
and to know the place for the first time.
—T. S. Eliot, "Little Gidding"

IMAGINE YOU ARE moving tomorrow. You have spent the last few weeks, and especially the last few days, organizing for the move, getting your things in order. In the process of packing, your whole life flashes before you. Here are photos of a much younger you with other kids from your high school days. Here is a packet of letters you have been carrying around for several years. Here is a plaque awarded you for high achievement from a company that went out of business a while ago. Here is a book, not yet read, a birthday present from a friend. What to take with you—what to leave behind?

While you are making piles of things to take and things to throw out, you may even sense a kind of redefining going on. You thought you knew who you were, but some of the items you have been sorting through seem to point to a different person entirely. Surely you are not the same person who collected these once practically sacred keepsakes. The throw-out pile grows; the take-with pile dwindles. Moving has given you the opportunity to assess your past and to decide how you want to create your future.

The journey you have embarked on from religion to personal spirituality is like that. For you to move ahead into a new spiritual understanding, there are times when you will want to sit down and decide which spiritual attitudes, concepts, and convictions to take along from your experience with religion, and which ones you must leave behind. You may have thought that leaving the faith of your childhood also means discarding everything you learned and believed, the worthwhile along with the worthless, while you were inside the walls of religion. But authentic spiritual truths, even those buried under heaps of dogmatic debris, belong to you, and you can claim them for your own personal spiritual path.

One of the most indelible memories of my eight years in monastic life was of the Christmas I celebrated as a novice. The novitiate year, or canonical year, as it is sometimes called—a year dictated by the church's canon law—is the first step to becoming a monk. It is a year of complete silence, retreat, study, contemplation, and work. Throughout the novitiate year, monks live the entire round of the Catholic liturgy to the fullest extent possible.

During my novitiate, our novice master, a pious, austere Bostonian, created a highly charged emotional Christmas experience for the young monks. We went to sleep at the unusually early hour of six on Christmas Eve. At eleven, the bell called us from our cells to the chapel. Dressed in our freshly pressed black robes, we filed slowly into the chapel in the dark, each with a lighted candle, chanting the Litany of the Saints in Latin. As we sat in the near darkness, two of the senior monks, dressed as acolytes, came out to the altar and began lighting what seemed like a forest of tall candles.

In the growing glow of the candles we could make out the majestic setting: the altar encircled with huge sprays of fresh flowers—this was the middle of winter in Indiana—and below it a crèche with Italianate figures of the Virgin Mary, Saint Joseph, the shepherds, and the angels. The chapel lights came on slowly, revealing more of the regal scene: a monk deacon holding a large, ornate missal, another swinging a thurible that sent up puffs of incense, another bearing a richly adorned silver container with holy water.

In the Catholic liturgy, Christmas is observed with not just one but three Masses. The first is celebrated at midnight, the second at dawn, and the third in the full light of morning. At exactly twelve o'clock, the start of the new day, the choir of monks intoned the moving chant from the psalms that begins the first Mass: *Dominus dixit ad me: Filius meus es tu, ego hodie genui te* ("You are my son, this day I have begotten you").

Kneeling there in the chapel, I was transfixed. It was as if my divine Source were speaking directly to me. I was God's son, born this day, every day. Years later, I would understand this

Discernment

profound sense of connection to be the real meaning behind the words of the psalm, which ancient liturgical authors applied only to the Christ child in this Christmas Mass. Billows of frankincense went up as the priest, a white-haired retired theology professor who was also one of our spiritual advisors, entered the sanctuary. He was dressed in gold-encrusted vestments and flanked by the two acolyte monks. From the choir above, Gregorian chant rose and fell like soothing waves on a sea of spiritual rapture.

Then came the reading from the gospels that linked this stirring moment in a monastery chapel with an event in time across two millennia: *In illo tempore: Exiit edictum a Caesare Augusto, ut describeretur universus orbis* ("And it came to pass in those days, that there went out a decree from Caesar Augustus, that all the world should be taxed").

As the Mass continued into the middle of the night, it took on a dreamlike quality. The flowers, the incense, the music, the candles, the Latin chant were intoxicating. For me, they supported an unforgettable mystical experience. After all these years, I still remember every detail of that splendid night, and how I felt as the drama unfolded.

When I left monastic life and the Catholic religion, my first impulse was to chuck everything. I stopped going to Mass on Sundays, stopped receiving the sacraments, stopped honoring special religious observances. I even broke some long-standing relationships over my total abandonment of the faith. But something came up that made me look more closely at what I was leaving behind, and what I might want to take with me from the past to forge a better spiritual way for myself in the future. Ironically, perhaps, the setting was again Christmas.

⟨ .. .. ⟩

I was living in Texas at the time, far away from my Ohio home-town. At Christmas, I went home to visit my family. It was my first Christmas there since I had left religion, and I knew it was going to be a touchy situation all around. From the beginning, the whole idea of the Christmas trip seemed illogical. Techni-cally, I was returning to my family to keep an observance in a religion of which I no longer considered myself a part. But Christmas, I reminded myself, was a special case. Less a reli-gious holiday, Christmas was a universal secular commemora-tion, an opportunity for giving and receiving gifts, renewing family bonds, and strengthening relationships with old friends.

Still, part of the Christmas ritual for our family was going to Midnight Mass together on Christmas Eve. In the days before Christmas, I went back and forth in my mind over whether or not to attend Mass with the family. I wanted desperately to stay true to my new convictions—matters of conscience I had arrived at after much soul searching. At the same time, I wanted to respect the faith of my family, particularly my devout parents.

I continued to weigh the pros and cons of joining the fam-ily at church right up to midnight, when I found myself roboti-cally standing, sitting, and kneeling through an uncomfortable Christmas Mass alongside my mother, my father, and my brother. I was doing Christmas again, following the same rich liturgy with the same words and measured moves, but now everything was different. I was no longer a believer.

There must be a lesson in all this, I thought. To be sure, there was. Did I have to throw out the baby of a transporting mystical experience with the bath water of organized religion?

Discernment

Once the Christmas season was over and I was back in my own home, I set aside some time to reflect on how I, as a nonreligious person, might show up at other religious functions such as weddings, funerals, christenings, and similar gatherings of family and friends. I wanted to honor them but still hold onto my inner feelings about my personal spirituality. More than that, could I find within those religious interludes something to bring into my new spiritual life?

I decided that, since I was making new spiritual guidelines for myself, I would go where my intuition guided me—even if it directed me back into a religious setting for a time. Whenever I reentered the perimeter of religion, I would do so as a gift of my presence to the people I cared about. I came to understand that I could embrace these shared public situations and also remain true to my private spiritual convictions.

Aside from honoring family or friends, there could be a further spiritual opportunity in occasionally revisiting the religious beliefs I had set aside like so much baggage I did not want to take with me on my new path. Sometimes, hidden within the literal renderings and skewed interpretations of organized religion, we find spiritual nuggets of great value. I think of this as a rescue mission—of excavating high truths buried beneath the structures of religion and bringing them into our new, personally realized spirituality.

Back from my rather wrenching Christmas trip to my hometown, I knew I had to find a way to incorporate at least part of my religious past into my evolving personal spiritual search. Not the pomp and splendor of Midnight Mass in a monastery, which was a unique event never to be duplicated, but the sense of connection I felt with the Source during that special night.

{ .. .. }

In sorting through my memories of the two Christmases—one as a young Catholic monk and the other as a fallen-away Catholic—I returned to the first words of the Introit for the First Mass at Christmas (*Dominus dixit ad me: Filius meus es tu*; "The Lord said to me, you are my son"). Religion teaches us that God is far off, perfect, and unattainable. We, on the other hand, are earthbound, imperfect, and unworthy of connecting with God. But here in this simple statement, imbedded in the Catholic Mass, taken from the centuries-old psalms of the Jewish King David, was a clue to help me to new awareness in my spiritual seeking. I could embrace the phrase and keep it as my own.

Christian religions teach us that God has only one son, Jesus Christ. But I too am a child of God, a son of God. The words of the psalmist King David must apply to me as much as to himself. Religious tradition later appropriated the psalm and its sentiments as a "prophesy" of the birth of Jesus, but the psalm seems to be saying that we are all entitled to claim sonship—primary connection—with the divine Source.

The great lesson I learned from attending Christmas Midnight Mass with my family after I left religion was this: the spiritual substance hidden there under piles of separation thinking and worthlessness programming was mine after all, and I could incorporate it into my life in my own way. I ended up bringing with me from Roman Catholicism this and many other great spiritual truths. They are truths that resonate not only with my thinking but with my intuition and my feelings. I have used these truths to help build my own spiritual life.

In deciding what to leave behind and what to take with you on your spiritual quest, you might consider going back and unraveling genuine sacred truths from the ball of string of religious rules and doctrines. Knowing what to rescue from your religious past is an ongoing process. Usually these spiritual nuggets simply reveal themselves if you put out the intention of retrieving them. You will know them when they arrive in your mind and heart.

You can push your search-and-rescue mission along by adopting a metaphorical way of thinking. In our materialistic culture, we tend to see everything one-dimensionally. You go out to your car in the morning and find the window on the driver's side broken in, glass shattered over the floor, and a large rock on the seat; you conclude that some minor vandalism occurred in your driveway. Most of us stop there. We want to know who did the deed, but for all practical purposes that is the end of it.

Seeing metaphorically invites us to explore another dimension of the event. If the materialistic approach is about *what* happened, the metaphorical approach is about *why* it happened. Behind the one-dimensional incident is the multidimensional meaning. In the example of the broken car window, you fill out a police report, call your insurance company, and get out the duct tape and plastic. But the event need not stop there.

There may be another way to read a bashed-in car window, other than as simply a senseless act of random violence. You have at least three metaphors to investigate: a car, a window, and a break-in. Because you are in your car every day, you could consider it a symbol of yourself. The window represents how you see the world. Perhaps the break-in means there is a break-through in how you view everything in your experience. The incident in the driveway suddenly becomes an opportunity to entertain the idea that a major insight, awareness, or sudden leap of consciousness is heading your way. Instead of regarding the apparent vandalism with feelings of fear, distrust, and annoy-ance, you begin to see it as a wake-up call to a new and exciting direction for your life.

This is metaphorical thinking, and it is an ally on your jour-ney to a self-made spiritual life. We humans used to be quite good at seeing and thinking in metaphors. One of my teachers, the eminent historian of philosophy Louis Mackey, used to say to his students on the subject of looking for multiple meanings under the obvious, "You must remember that Western man learned to read by reading the Bible." For centuries, the Guten-berg Bible, printed in Germany in the 1450s, was the only deposi-tory of written language widely available. People learning to read with the Bible as their textbook grasped what they were reading on many levels beyond the literal. While they were absorbing the words, they also were coming into contact with the metaphori-cal, symbolic, and allegorical meanings behind them.

But the facility of bringing many possible meanings to a sin-gle word or event did not begin on the cusp of the Renaissance. It has always been part of human nature. The ancients lived in two parallel worlds, the one they could experience with the physical senses and the one they could imagine. The world of the imagination was considered more valuable than the see-and-touch here and now.

Discernment

Our ability to look for meaning past what we could see and touch was obscured with the rise of rationalism in the seventeenth century and all but lost during the Industrial Revolution and the dawn of modern times. Although there are some indications the pendulum is swinging back into balance, we are for the most part stuck in the place where one event equals one meaning. The car window is smashed in; call the police; call the insurance company; end of story.

You and I live under the tyranny of the literal. Reading only one meaning into things is terribly limiting, especially when we are looking for spiritual truths. If we take a literal approach and say that Adam and Eve were real people who lived a few thousand years ago (down the declensions outlined in the Bible of who begat whom), then we are missing out on the possibility of seeing the Genesis creation story as a fascinating myth about the emergence of the human species from the garden of a luxuriant and generous planet. Go further, and you can see it as a parable of the human illusion of separation or the Fall from our divine Source.

To insist on a literal interpretation of the Adam and Eve story leaves us in the difficult position of having to prove the absurd, untenable idea that humans appeared on the scene a mere few thousand years ago. Indisputable archeological evidence shows that we have been here for at least two million, perhaps as long as four million years. More than that, the literal reading prevents us from exploring the mysterious messages hidden behind the narrative, depriving us of the lessons in a profound spiritual story. In this case, it also diminishes the real dramatic saga of our species evolving upward through ever-higher realms of self-awareness.

Most Christian thinkers now reject the literal explanation of our creation as set down in the Bible. Here and there, you will find a preacher going on about Adam and Eve as if they were as close to him in time as his own great-grandparents, and how God created the world in six days. But mainstream religion recognizes our origin myth as just that, a parable about our human beginning. Science has helped us in this regard; the more indisputable facts we uncover about our history on the planet, the less relevant are the Biblical explanations.

Still, literal rendering of so-called revealed spiritual truth persists in the world's religions, and it continues to spell trouble for the rest of us. If you cling to the letter of the first commandment of the Mosaic Law ("I am the Lord thy God; thou shalt have no other Gods before me") all believers in their own God are heretics, and you must stamp them out. "A literal reading of the Old Testament," Sam Harris reminds us in *The End of Faith*, "not only permits, but requires heretics to be put to death."

This craziness is not part of our distant, benighted human past, when armies slaughtered each other and lands were laid waste over whose God was God. Unfortunately, it is as chillingly contemporary as the most recent suicide bombing of innocent people in the name of God. A man steals into an abortion clinic in Florida and shoots down a doctor because, in his mind, the Bible says "Thou shalt not kill," and the doctor was murdering human fetuses. A group of townspeople in Saudi Arabia form

88

a circle, pick up stones, and close in on an eighteen-year-old girl who was raped. After all, does the Holy Scripture not tell us that we must not commit adultery?

These are demented examples of literal religious thinking, and most of us recognize and condemn them as such. But they serve to remind us of the trap inherent in subscribing to the exact word of religious truth so called. If we get caught in the trap, we miss extraordinary opportunities to explore the real truth that fosters our spiritual growth. For hundreds of years, Biblical historians and theologians have argued over exactly when and where the Red Sea parted, allowing the ancient Hebrews to flee their slave masters in Egypt. Confined by their literal thinking, they overlooked the dramatic metaphor of personal transformation from the bondage of the human condition—believing ourselves to be separate from our Source—to the Promised Land of new spiritual awareness.

As you scan your inventory of religious beliefs, I encourage you to go for the metaphorical. All the great spiritual teachers, from Buddha and Jesus to Confucius and the Zen masters, speak to us in parables, symbols, similes, and riddles. Their sayings are rich in figures of speech, inviting us into a mystical realm far away from the dry and brittle literal. Rather than dismissing all the concepts you learned and believed in organized religion, consider looking at them for their authentic spiritual content, and use them in your continuing search.

Sometimes spiritual truths emerge from your religious indoctrination quite suddenly and effortlessly. More often, you have to make an effort to see past what has been staring you in the face for years in order to use it on a spiritual path that makes sense to you. When I taught myself how to read the old articles of faith as metaphors, it opened a whole new world for me.

{ .. .. }

Once again, Christmas. The Christian churches celebrate the birth of Jesus, but you can use the occasion to contemplate the birth of new spiritual awareness in yourself. The Divine Child is an archetype alive in each of us. Christmas can activate this archetype in such a way that it becomes a personal spiritual unfolding. Likewise for the celebration of Easter, commemorating the resurrection of Jesus from the dead. Whether or not you believe in the supposed actual event two millennia ago, you can take its meaning to yourself and see it as a raising of merely human awareness to an understanding of your essential spiritual nature.

An electrifying moment in the New Testament is when Jesus, preaching to thousands of people out in the country, is told that his listeners are hungry. He raises his eyes heavenward in thanksgiving and then has his students distribute their own meager lunch—five loaves of bread and two fish. Five thousand people eat and are filled, and the students collect several baskets of leftovers. You do not have to believe in miracles, in Jesus, or the New Testament to get the spiritual lesson in this remarkable event. Abundance is our birthright, and when we acknowledge the Source of our supply what we need comes rushing into our experience.

In seeking eternal truths from traditional religion, I made some surprising discoveries that pushed me along on my personal path. With Jewish friends, I went to a synagogue for Rosh

Hashanah, the Jewish New Year, where I heard the flat, thunderous sound of the shofar, or ram's horn, announcing the beginning of a new time. For me, it became a personal wake-up cry to rededicate myself to my spiritual aspirations. The apples dipped in honey, which are part of the custom on that day, symbolized the sweetness of the search for connection with the Source.

Judaism appealed to me on the mystical level. Even though it is the origin and stronghold of the judging sky-king monotheism that I found increasingly difficult to relate to, there were other concepts and customs to appreciate. Passover commemorates the passing over of the Angel of Death on the eve of fleeing Egypt. Bitter herbs are eaten, as they were the night before the ancient Hebrews undertook their journey of freedom. I understood the solemn memorial as an allegory of the human journey to the Promised Land of higher spiritual consciousness. As little as possible is to be taken on that journey. We need to leave our old ideas and attitudes behind. The passage may be arduous, thus the bitter herbs, but the rewards of divine connection at the end of our wandering are immense.

Christian religions begin in the observance of Passover. Jesus himself used the occasion to teach his students the higher meaning of the event, the spiritual lesson of life as a journey the human soul is making back to its Source. I found much to admire in this stirring tradition and eagerly added it to my own spiritual way of thinking. Even now, when Passover comes around in the spring, I look forward to an invitation to a Seder, the Passover meal, to contemplate the mysteries it embraces.

Islam did not hold out as many fascinations for me as the more familiar Judeo-Christian teachings of my upbringing, but I was able to relate to Ramadan, the ninth month of the Islamic calendar, which is given over to fasting and reflection. All teachers of spiritual wisdom point to the idea of retreat as a necessary interior practice. The Buddha fasted forty-nine days as he meditated under the Bodhi Tree; Jesus fasted forty days in the desert before beginning his public ministry; the prophet Elijah fasted forty days as well; and Moses fasted eighty days before receiving the divine laws atop Mt. Sinai. I found that taking a few days of retreat at the time of Ramadan, usually in the late autumn of the year, was a way to participate spiritually in an uplifting activity observed at the same time by about one billion of my fellow humans, a sixth of the world's population.

In no way did I ever consider myself a believer in any of those religions. However, taking some of their traditions as metaphors, I was able to internalize the seed of their spiritual truth and feel supported on my own journey of the spirit.

} .. .. {

In all the religions I encountered in my search, I found prayer to be one of the fundamental elements of the canon. Prayer is particularly problematic for the seeker who has turned away from organized religion. Should you pray? If so, whom do you pray to? The God of the monotheistic religions does not reign in some far-off heaven anymore, dispensing or withholding favors. If you pray to some substitute, such as the Great Spirit or the Universe, are you simply using stand-in words for what you and everyone else knows is the G— word?

When I left religion, prayer became a pressing issue. Besides holding a dominant position in organized religions, it is part of

our language and cultural customs. The person next to you
sneezes, and you say, "God bless you!" It is a prayer to God,
asking for heavenly assistance on your behalf. In all life's crises,
prayers are present. Someone dies, and you send the family a
card with the message that you are praying for them. An accident happens and you pray that no one is hurt. We even have
national days of prayer to meet national crises.

Prayer is tied inextricably to God, of course, whatever you
call him or however you conceive of him. Prayer is pleading for
a good thing we do not have, whether it is the safety of a child
going off to college or a reprieve from illness, good luck on an
exam or a closing on a house. In prayer, we make a petition to
God, or Whomever, to give us some benefit we believe we do not
possess—but that God, or Whoever, does possess. To understand
the cosmology behind prayer, we have to return to the God-as-
king model of spirituality. God, in far-off heaven, has everything. I need or want some things. I ask God to give me those
things. The Lord's Prayer, we saw, is the embodiment of that
paradigm—a withholding lord, a deprived and suppliant vassal.

Many modern seekers are exploring the place of prayer in
personal spirituality. Larry Dossey, in *Healing Words: The Power
of Prayer and the Practice of Medicine* and other excellent books,
cites the impressive evidence that prayer can positively influence
the health of body and mind. But whether those prayers are
effective because they go to God or because they come from the
loving, blessing hearts of the people praying is anybody's guess.

Creating your own spiritual way, you have to decide if you
want to believe there is a God somewhere withholding something from you. Early on in my journey from religion to personal

spirituality, I began to entertain the idea that God was not out there but in here—in me—and that God was not holding anything back from my experience. It was the seed of a belief that, with constant reality checks, eventually became rooted in my spiritual awareness. Because there was no God outside myself withholding good things from me, there did not seem to be a logic or a purpose to traditional forms of prayer.

I found an approach to the problem of prayer, and it has served me well through the years. I exchanged the old idea of prayer as petitioning God with a simple blessing from me. If God is in me, in my heart and mind, in my very being, then anyone or anything I bless receives all the good God has to give. I look upon something or someone and I bless. Anything beyond that seems to me to be mere superstition rooted in illogical belief.

This manner of prayer has worked well for me in private and public situations. In private, I am able to send good wishes from my mind and heart. I often do this in response to a friend or family member who asks me to pray for him or her. I did, but it had nothing to do with asking God for something. In public, at a wedding or a funeral, where I am invited to pray for the happy couple or the soul of the deceased, I use the time to reflect on them, thank them for being in my life, and give them my blessing.

Prayer, if you reframe it to accommodate your new spiritual awareness, can be a powerful support to the path you are forging for yourself, and a basic demonstration of it. Whenever the request or the impulse to pray comes to you, stop for a moment. Do you want to implore a far-off God handed down to you as the truth of your creative Source? Do you believe there is a God out there holding back what you need if you are to fulfill your human potential, refusing to give it to you?

How, then, will you redefine prayer to make it meaningful to you? If there is no God on a heavenly throne denying you happiness, health, prosperity, creativity, peace of mind, freedom, joy, and all the other good things of life—no God keeping these good things back from your family, your friends, your coworkers, everyone in your life, all living beings on the planet—then how do you pray?

Consider blessing from the awareness that all you or anyone else needs or wants, you and they already have from a boundless, bountiful, and generous Source. In this way, what began as a desperate appeal to an imaginary being above the clouds becomes a full-hearted expression of gratitude.

There is only one prayer: the prayer of thanksgiving.

CHAPTER SIX

obstacles

The greatest foes, and whom we must chiefly combat,
are within.

—Miguel de Cervantes, *Don Quixote*

IN THE MIDST OF seeking an authentic personal spirituality for myself, I returned to the Dachau concentration camp near Munich in southern Germany. I had never been there before, but I say I returned because of what was going to be revealed to me as my search took me ever deeper into my soul's history.

A time comes, as you explore the amazing possibilities of a personal spiritual path, when you are compelled by the inexorable momentum of the search itself to go into areas of the spirit you never imagined when you began the sacred process. After answering the call to find your creative Source on your own, you questioned everything you were taught and sincerely looked into your innermost beliefs. You determined what was valuable from the old religious way of framing your spiritual life, and what you needed to leave behind. Now you find yourself in a fascinating place, which I like to think of as a kind of final clearing stage for building your new, self-made spirituality.

Here you are likely to come up against the greater cosmic questions of who you truly are, where you came from, where you are going, and what you are doing on this planet in the first place. You may have begun your search for your Source with a version of those questions, but now they seem to be the curious musings of a child. Suddenly, there is a leap into the vast reaches of multidimensionality, a sense of the hugeness of your soul and its workings through time—perhaps through many lifetimes— gathering information, learning lessons, and expanding its awareness on your journey back to the Creator.

Along the road to personal spirituality, I found there are no short cuts. For several years, freed of my religious yoke, I thought I could pursue my spiritual aspirations without paying much attention to well-being in other parts of myself. I assumed that my mental and emotional health were separate and apart from my spiritual seeking. If I concentrated on my spiritual quest, I thought, all those other things would take care of them- selves or be taken care of by God. But even as I seemed to progress in building a spiritual life for myself, I watched as I slowly spiraled down into unhappiness toward a deepening and chronic depression.

Now I understand that we live in several bodies at once. The most obvious is the physical body, but there is also a mental or psychological body, an emotional body, and a spiritual body. There may be many more layers of our human reality, but these at least are the ones of which we have some direct experience at this point in our evolution. While I was working so hard to advance my spiritual life, I allowed my emotional and psychological bodies to fall increasingly out of balance with the rest of me. It was a classic case of what I learned later is called the "spiritual bypass," an attempt to forge a personal spirituality without going through the process of healing the wounded psychological and emotional parts of myself.

The late Buddhist master Chogyam Trungpa may have been the first to name it the spiritual bypass: using spiritual practices to try to step over unassimilated childhood experiences and other painful biographical events. In a spiritual bypass, you try to treat your out-of-balance thoughts and behaviors by going to the spiritual realm through prayer, meditation, or other spiritual practices. We imagine that God will take care of this depression, this phobia, this guilt complex, this eating disorder, this toxic family dynamic, this chronic physical aliment. The angels will fly down from heaven and dissolve my anger, my anxiety, my feelings of loneliness and alienation, the pain left from my early-life traumas. But of course it does not work. Psychological and emotional wounds need to be addressed at their own level. If they are left unhealed, the progress of your spiritual development eventually slows to a halt and breaks down—and then it may seem that nothing can save you from the distress you are feeling, not even God or the angels.

Obstacles

Well into my own spiritual bypass, I was enjoying a successful public life. A respected film critic with both an extensive academic background and experience in Hollywood moviemaking,
I was asked to establish a film school at a prestigious private college in Santa Fe. It was the chance of a lifetime, and I threw
myself into it with enormous energy and creativity. Nine students signed up for the program's first semester; a year later,
the number tripled. After six years, two hundred film majors
had been added to the college's up-to-then sagging enrollment
figures. Students in the film program brought to the college not
only numbers and tuition revenues (they represented about a
quarter of the school's total population and income) but origi-
nality and imagination, such that the entire institution seemed
to be revitalized.

While I was regularly appearing in the media and taking
pleasure in the adulation of my students and colleagues, pri-
vately I was lonely, anxious, and miserable. My spiritual search
continued on course, as I attended one personal growth workshop after another and pursued various esoteric teachings with
self-proclaimed masters, but I was profoundly unhappy. Deep
inside, I knew my avoidance of the necessary and difficult psychological and emotional work, my spiritual bypass, was not
working.

Depression hung on me like a heavy old winter coat. I spent
more time sleeping or trying to sleep; I isolated myself, walking
from room to room of my house brooding and preoccupied.
Eventually, the depression began to intrude into my work life.
I was hardly able to get myself to my office at the college; once
there, I spent most of the day in a somber, gloomy mood.

After procrastinating for a few weeks, I decided to seek the help of a traditional therapist. Fortunately, I found a gifted Jungian analyst who had recently moved to Santa Fe. Sabine Lucas was a graduate of Heidelberg University and the C. G. Jung Institute in Zurich—academic credentials that appealed to me as the chair of my own academic department. Sabine was sympathetic, as well, with the kind of eclectic spiritual path I was formulating for myself outside religion. As I got to know her, I discovered that she was opened to the paranormal through personal experiences while living in England. She also had translated two books of the American trance medium Jane Roberts, *Seth Speaks* and *The Nature of Personal Reality,* into German. In spiritual matters, she was well outside traditional religious practice; she followed the teachings of the contemporary Indian avatar, Sri Sathya Sai Baba.

My therapy, based on Jungian dream analysis, began in the usual way, with self-revelation down through many tiers of my emotional and psychological life. The dreams were about my parents, my childhood, my early school years. Everything in our weekly sessions was what could be called textbook therapy: locating and releasing the residue from disturbing events in the past that I had carried in me for a long time, and that finally had devolved into unrelenting depression.

One morning, less than a month after beginning therapy, I woke with a start, trying to retain the end of a disturbing dream image: a bleak, bone-cold winter night with snow all around, a winding mountain road, trees with bare branches, piercing headlights from an old German car. All that day a feeling of hopelessness and confusion clung to me. There seemed to be nothing to hang the dream image onto. By that evening, I was guessing that the feeling was a reflection of my inner state at that time; in a way, I felt as isolated and alienated as a person in that bleak landscape. I almost feared going to sleep and possibly facing what might be behind those ghostly headlights.

Sabine immediately recognized the dream as a past-life memory and told me so. I had no way of knowing, but was soon to learn, that she had extensive experience with past-life dreams. The minute she said "past life," something in me leapt up. From that point on, the dreams took a dramatic turn. A few nights later, I had a dream about going into the dusty storage room of an antique shop and searching around for something. There were old trunks and stacks of papers and old phonograph records, and a large journal book written in German, which in the dream I understood but in waking life did not. This richly detailed dream was different from the impressionistic bits and pieces I had been excavating and assembling up to then as a picture of my early psychological life.

Sabine said she believed the dream of my rummaging around the old storage room—my soul's storage room, where all the records from previous lifetimes were kept—signaled that I was ready to examine that lifetime and see how its lessons might relate to my present life situation. Soon, more of these dreams, with allusions to a past in Germany, arrived, begging for our attention.

Sabine explained to me how to recognize past-life recall among the many dreams that come up from the unconscious, even if the dreamer does not remember them fully or at all— four of them every night, on average, over a thousand of them in a year. Briefly, ordinary dreams are made up of swatches of experience from waking life and shown to us as a kaleidoscope of inner pictures in symbolic form. They usually relate directly to what we are processing in daily life at the time. For instance, you might have a scary dream about being mugged and your wallet stolen; it relates to a waking-life situation in which you feel someone is talking about you behind your back, stealing your good reputation.

Past-life memories are different. They unfold, most often, as a movie story does, with more narrative continuity. The characters are dressed in the clothes of the past, the furniture is old-fashioned, the landscape seems to be of another country or from another time. In an ordinary dream, the unconscious takes random pictures from the past or present, shuffles them up like a deck of cards, and then spreads them out for us to read as a kind of bulletin written in symbols. There are more ways of differentiating up-to-the-minute dreams from past-life dreams, but the clinical information is sketchy, because traditional psychoanalysts typically avoid dealing with past lives at all, preferring to interpret the unusual storylike pictures in the same way they read ordinary dream images, using the language of symbols. Sabine's recent book on the subject, *Bloodlines of the Soul: Karmic Patterns in Past Life Dreams,* outlines her research, presents spellbinding case studies, and breaks new ground in this regard.

Past-life work was not entirely unfamiliar to me. Early in my spiritual search, I studied briefly with Shirley MacLaine's past-life teacher, Chris Griscom, who was exploring reincarnation memories through bodywork. After several sessions, some

of what might have been my soul's long history through time
emerged. But none of the "lives" seemed to relate to anything
in my present experience, so I lost interest and moved on.

My religious upbringing made me somewhat skeptical of
past lives. The Catholic Church teaches against reincarnation,
considering each person to have a unique soul that is working its
way toward a final, moment-after-death eternal punishment or
reward. I discovered later that the church's stand on past lives
was not always so unilateral. Up to the Second Council of Constantinople in 553 A.D., Christian theologians held a broader
definition of the soul, one that included the living of many lives
through time. I was entirely open to the possibility, and as more
"German" dreams surfaced from the depths of my unconscious
I was faced with mounting evidence for having lived at least one
time before.

⟩ .. .. ⟨

In forty-seven highly detailed dreams over the next five years,
I "remembered" a full and extraordinary life my soul had experienced before I was born into my present lifetime. The dreams
were sprinkled out over the entire half-decade of my work with
Sabine, without a clear chronology. Each dream seemed to surface from my unconscious at a time when a similar set of circumstances was coming up in my waking life. For more than
a year into the process, it was not at all clear exactly how the
whole lifetime looked. Nor was it clear why I was remembering
it. Folded in with the dreams from the German lifetime were
many others—some of them as long and dramatic as epic
movies. None of them appeared to be connected to the past

life that continued to interject itself with increasing urgency into my therapy.

The first dream in the past-life cycle turned out to be the one that compelled me to seek a therapist. Not surprisingly, as I learned later, it was a memory of the end of that life. I was driven up a desolate mountain road in the middle of a bitterly cold winter's night. German SS soldiers pulled me out of a car and led me, hands bound behind my back, to a clump of bushes. They stepped away as another soldier cocked a gun and shot me in the head. My last memory was of staring like a terrified, paralyzed rabbit into the glaring headlights from the car, illuminating the impromptu site of my execution. I was a woman.

The dreams arrived out of order. In one, I was a ten-year-old girl in a dance class to which a youthful Adolf Hitler paid a visit. A few nights later, I was in my midtwenties, making alarming discoveries in a Nazi concentration camp. In the next dream, I was a girl again, being inducted into the Hitler Youth service. Over time, with Sabine's guidance and her firsthand experience of Germany during those times, I was able to put together a chronological line that made some sense.

My name was Hilde. I was born into an upper-middle-class family in Germany around 1918, just before or after the end of the First World War. I grew up in a strict household and was instructed in conventional bourgeois German values. In spite of the shortages and rationing, the punishing inflation, and other difficulties of the period, I was offered a few modest opportunities for personal refinement, including piano and dance lessons.

At one of the dance lessons, in the upstairs loft of an old building, young Adolf Hitler made an appearance, probably courting votes for his National Socialist Party. Apparently, he was an acquaintance of my dance teacher. She was at least familiar enough with him to ask for his financial support of her fine arts school. I watched spellbound as Hitler declined assistance, encouraging her to trust in God for the success of her efforts (remarkable counsel if we remember the ungodly atrocities that would be committed under his future leadership). His presence was absolutely magnetic. In the dream, I felt my heart thumping wildly as I looked at him.

Later, along with my school friends, I joined the Hitler Youth. In my late teens, I studied the new art of filmmaking and showed a particular interest in documentaries. By then, the Hitler regime was in power in the country. Excitement and a sense of promise were in the air, stoked by bold new political awareness. I attempted to avoid any involvement in politics but stepped unexpectedly into the maelstrom when documentary footage that I shot was screened for Hitler and his paramour, Eva Braun. The film's images of war refugees brought out Fräulein Braun's sympathetic side, precipitating a spat between them. Realizing I had witnessed both the refugee crisis and the couple's argument over it, and therefore probably knew too much, Braun turned on me and threatened dreadful consequences if I should ever tell anyone about what I had seen.

I must have breached the confidence of that encounter, because I was summoned with my mother to Gestapo headquarters in Berlin for interrogation. My punishment, no doubt presented as a privilege, was to serve the Reich in a special way as a member of the SS, Hitler's praetorian guard, the Nazi elite. The order must have been final and immediate, because in the next sequence of dreams, I was being trained to be an *Aufseherin,* a female guard in one of the Nazi concentration camps. After an excruciating round of instruction, I was assigned to the camp at Dachau, a few kilometers outside of Munich and put in charge of the women prisoners.

My dreams of the horrific life in the camp were wrenching, emotionally and physically draining. For several months, I wished the dream memories would simply go away and leave me in peace. Evenings I took sleep medication, thinking I might be able to numb myself past the ordeal. But Hilde's lifetime insistently pushed its way through my increasing dosage of seda-tives. In my waking hours, I was nervous and irritable; I was beginning to make bad decisions in my personal life and at work. I was like a man haunted.

In my restless sleep, dream visions surfaced of medical experiments conducted on petrified prisoners. I saw every detail—the white-coated doctor in charge standing with nurses around a seated, strapped-in prisoner-patient. When Sabine and I tried to understand why my recall of these grisly episodes was so precise—I could describe chrome-plated medical instruments to their exact measurements, for instance—we found a shocking clue in one dream. In the corner of the room, there was a movie camera. In addition to duties of prison matron, as a former doc-umentary filmmaker I was put to work meticulously recording these insane, inhumane experiments in the name of medical research.

The Hilde lifetime, so active in my sleep, cast a cheerless cloud over my waking days. Impatient for the dreams to end, I looked for some way of exorcising the demon that seemed to have attached itself to me. Taking the idea of exorcism literally, I sorted through my past religious baggage and went to a Catholic church in Santa Fe and had a Mass said for the repose of Hilde's soul. Kneeling there in my pew, listening to the priest say her name at the altar, I imagined having to explain to someone exactly what I was doing at that moment. The apparent absurdity of it all sent a chill through me. Here I was, having a Mass said for the soul of someone I believed was me in a previous lifetime, a Mass for my own soul. Such was the level of my confusion and desperation trying to deal with this pressing unfinished business.

The Mass and other bypasses around the issue, including ritually writing down and burning all the Hilde dreams under a tree in Sabine's yard, failed to put a stop to the dream story, which continued to arrive in installments like a serial puzzle. Part of me, caught in curiosity, awaited the dreams eagerly, if only to see whether the cycle was about to end. I would not know what the entire lifetime was, or what it meant for my present life, until all the pieces were in and I could string them together into something meaningful. Another part of me, exhausted from the ordeal, wanted the dreams to cease entirely.

I wish I could describe adequately the sense of terror that infused these past-life memories. In the dreams, Hilde feels squeezed in a vice, with her demanding SS superiors pressing in on her from one side and the prisoners under her charge plotting against her on the other. Fellow officers introduce her to some of the camp's more sordid underground activities, like a sexual "farm" devoted to sadism, mutilation, and other forms of degradation. Repulsed by these appalling goings-on, she is shunned by some of her peers. Then, fearing that she may be

thought of as an outsider, or too lenient, she hardens herself
against her prisoners, courting dreadful reprisals from them.

Earlier I spoke of the spiritual bypass; trying to settle emotional and psychological issues by giving them over to God or
by some other spiritual remedy does not work. You undoubtedly
have met many otherwise sincere seekers with obvious mental
and emotional obstruction to balance in their lives. Instead of
acknowledging and healing their wounds, they pretend that the
work is not necessary and that everything is already perfect, if
only they believe hard enough. True, perfection is already here
in the world of spirit, but meanwhile we are on a human journey in the flesh, which requires more mundane attention. If you
cut your leg, you clean the cut and bind it up; you do not putter
around the kitchen, putting on another pot of tea, as you bleed
to death.

While I was reliving the Hilde lifetime in my dreams, I
understood that I was working through emotional and psychological barriers preventing me from proceeding further on my
path to an authentic spirituality. Until I dealt with the issues
brought up by the memories of my soul's most recent past, I
could not live a life in balance—a life of connection with my
divine Source.

{ .. .. }

At last, four years after the first Hilde dream, surrendering to
the soul-mending process utterly, I planned a trip to Germany,
to Munich, to Dachau. I was determined to piece together the
entire Hilde lifetime so that I could try to comprehend its soul
lesson and meaning for the life I was living now. If I could stand

in the place where Hilde had stood, I thought, see what she saw, felt what she felt, it all would be made clear.

These were dark days. Something in me had reason to hope because, for the first time, I sensed that the end of my search was in sight. But the prospect of having to face the scene of the horrors coming up in my past-life memories kept me in a constant state of anxiety.

I say dark days; I am reminded of the book by the Spanish mystic Saint John of the Cross, *The Dark Night of the Soul.* John was a sixteenth-century poet, mystic, priest, and monk, a member of Teresa of Avila's Discalced Carmelite Order, the Barefoot Carmelites, committed to reform of the Carmelites during the chaotic times of the Inquisition. In the book (a twenty-six-chapter commentary on a shimmering, beautiful, and sensual eight-verse poem), John addresses those who encounter despair in their spiritual search. He urges them to risk entering the dark night, where the Source seems to have left them, to feel the feelings of desolation, abandonment, and dislocation. In this way, the seeker becomes a spiritual blank slate, which John believed was a prerequisite for true connection with the divine.

What makes the dark night dark is the fear that the spiritual seeker has become lost on the path. No spiritual feeling comes, no assurance that what has been undertaken is bearing fruit. The inner landscape is a desert through which the seeker trudges looking for some indication that there has been a purpose and meaning to all the noble efforts—efforts that seem to have come to naught.

The Dark Night of the Soul has been a consolation to spiritual aspirants for four hundred years. Just knowing that feeling aban-

doned by God is a step on the way to an authentic personal spirituality can be a comfort. Psychological states approaching despair
appear to be part of the process of seeking the Source. Far from
considering these states as obstacles to the search for divine connection, John of the Cross thought of them as a kind of blessing:

> O guiding Night,
> O Night more lovely than Dawn,
> O Night that has united the lover with his beloved
> Transforming the Lover in her Beloved.

I arrived in Munich in the second week of December. When
I asked how to get to Dachau, I was surprised to find that it was
close enough to the city to be a stop on the municipal transport
system. Maybe, I thought, with this proximity to a large urban
center, Dachau was not the nightmare slaughterhouse I had
dreamed about. My optimism evaporated the minute I stepped
off the train and began walking toward the camp, which is today
a World War II memorial site. Approaching the stark brick walls,
I understood immediately how isolated this place must have
been, even within the busy town. Later I was told that when the
camp was occupied townspeople were forbidden to ask about
what was going on just over the walls; they were often arrested
and imprisoned for even glancing in the direction of the camp.

Hitler became chancellor of Germany on January 30, 1933.
Six weeks later, the Dachau concentration camp opened to
house as many as fifty thousand enemies of the Third Reich,
which included at first political prisoners from the Munich
area—Social Democrats and Communists, along with Catholic

priests and Jewish doctors and lawyers. By the start of the war, in 1939, it was a prison for anyone the government considered undesirable: primarily Jews, but also, gypsies, homosexuals, and others. Over the twelve years of its operation, a quarter of a million prisoners were registered at Dachau; the total dead—by torture, hanging, firing squad, starvation, and gassing—may never be known. Soviet prisoners of war were executed by the thousands immediately upon their arrival within the walls.

An unrelenting and chilling drizzle fell from a dense, colorless sky the day I visited Dachau. *Grau und regnerisch,* the Germans say; "gray and rainy." Even before I walked through the entrance, I began to feel numb, as if walking in a trance. Above me, the huge iron gate was emblazoned with the words *Arbeit Macht Frei* (Work Makes Us Free), the sadistically ironic phrase the Nazis put over the gates of their concentration camps. No matter how hard camp prisoners worked, the only freedom they were released into was death.

I toured the old administration building, which now was a museum, spending a long time staring at photographs of prisoners undergoing medical experiments. Had I taken those photos? Then out to the treeless grounds, where once stood hundreds of rows of barracks and outbuildings. I visited the so-called camp crematorium, an incinerator, really, where the bodies of dead prisoners were burned. The camp guidebook said that when the American Seventh Army liberated Dachau at the end of April 1945, more than two thousand bodies had been left stacked here against the crematorium walls awaiting disposal.

I moved in slow motion, plodding heavily across the wide, empty fields, which had been the stage for so much terror, anguish, and death. Although I entered the camp with about two dozen other people, I now saw only six or seven meandering around the walkways. Time was sluggish. Eventually, as the afternoon wore on to a premature evening, I was the only person in the camp. Unfeeling, unthinking, weighted down by the misty rain and the metallic clouds, I proceeded like a sleepwalker out the barbed-wire-encrusted gate. When I glanced at my watch, I was stunned to see that I had spent more than six hours walking nonstop around the camp. To this day, I do not know how I got back to my hotel. Suddenly, it seemed, I was in my room, in bed, sinking into a deep sleep.

If I was expecting a sudden epiphany, an answer to all my questions about Hilde's life and death and its significance for the present, it was not provided by the visit to Dachau. But in the next year more dreams would surface to complete the past-life picture. In one key dream, I watched a cart loaded down with very large dead rats being transported through a street in a medieval town (Dachau is a preserved medieval town). One supposed rat falls from the back of the cart, which now has become a truck, and tries to run away. It is not a rat at all, but a beggar boy. Sabine's interpretation was that Hilde was no longer seeing the prisoners as vermin that needed to be exterminated but as human beings.

The dream represented an enormous shift in consciousness and resulted in a heart opening that ultimately would be Hilde's undoing. Fellow SS guards denounced her for being too soft on the prisoners and blamed her for causing an escape. She was brought before the camp police for a humiliating and brutal interrogation that lasted several hours into the winter night.

Obstacles

112

Then she was handcuffed and stuffed into the back of an old Duesenberg, driven to a remote location, shot in the head, and dumped down a snowy embankment.

At last, all the pieces were there. Now a meaning emerged. In a former lifetime, I had given myself over to hero worship of a charismatic individual and out of loyalty to him was led to commit unspeakable crimes against other people. In the midst of carrying out these atrocities, I experienced a conversion and tried to mitigate some of the torments I had caused. For my awakening to humanity, to compassion, I was killed.

But what did this mean for my present lifetime? Hilde died in December 1941. When I was born into this lifetime nine months later, I came in with a huge spiritual debt; the Eastern religions call it karma. Unaware of my recent soul history, I began to pay off that debt by entering a monastery and devoting myself to prayer, contemplation, fasting, and silence. After I left monastic life, I continued my attachment to the parts of it that kept me isolated and fearful. Living a life of self-denial, I was depriving myself of loving relationships, financial security, and all the other good things I was meant to enjoy as a human expression of my divine Source.

Emotional and psychological fallout from the Hilde lifetime held me back from moving further in my spiritual search. I was lost in the dark night. Through the therapeutic process with Sabine, that lifetime and its themes came into full awareness and integrated into my present life, allowing me to advance to the next step, into the higher realms of myself. A few years after we excavated the lifetime, Sabine wrote her book *Bloodlines of the Soul*. One chapter retells the Hilde story from her point of view, as a psychoanalyst. For me, it marked the definitive end of that lifetime and its influence on my present life.

There is no substitute for the sometimes hard work of healing the wounds of the past—and that includes the far distant past of the soul, if necessary. Ignoring those wounds, suppressing them, pretending they are not there delays or sidetracks, or otherwise sabotages, the search for an authentic personal spirituality. I encourage you to explore all the shadowy areas of your mind and heart as part of your spiritual search. The dark night will yield to the clear light of a new spiritual dawn.

With my most recent soul lessons behind me, I embarked on another phase of my spiritual adventure. To my complete surprise, three rock-solid values from monastic life would become the building blocks of my new spirituality. They were values I had lived within the monastery walls that had been for me so much a mirror of the walls of Hilde's Dachau. I recovered them from the rubble of my religious past to create a mature spiritual life on my own. In the next three chapters, I share them with you.

PART THREE

building

CHAPTER SEVEN

detachment

It is possible to be a solitary in one's mind while living in a crowd, and it is possible for one who is a solitary to live in the crowd of his own thoughts.

—AMMA SYNCLETICA, DESERT MOTHER, THIRD CENTURY A.D.

WHAT IF YOU woke tomorrow morning, cleaned up, brushed your teeth, and then went to your closet for your clothes—and instead of finding neat rows of your usual outfits you saw hanging there only a pair of black slacks, a white T-shirt, and a religious habit? The habit is a black robe with room at the neck for a Roman collar and buttons down the front from the neck to the feet. A black rope with black tassels goes around the waist and completes the garment.

For eight years, that was how my day began. My life was one of contemplation, work, solitude, silence, and study. Behind monastery walls, I lived in community with other monks, own-ing nothing but sharing everything in common—in a perfect communistic system. In place of intimate relationships, I had the warm camaraderie of the other monks. When I was needed at another of the monastery's religious houses, I went without question at a moment's notice.

After I left monastic life, the transition to "normal" life was difficult at first. Rising at the same time, going to bed at the same time, wearing the same attire, and interacting almost exclusively with people who were maintaining the same lifestyle created in me a structure that was not easy to shake off. Gradually, though, I drifted back into what we all consider ordinary living. But I tried to keep the spirit of the monastery alive within me in some way. Many aspects of being a monk, I realized, could serve me as a spiritual seeker, whether I lived inside the walls or outside them. I could be *in* the world, but not *of* the world.

{ .. .. }

Over the years since my experience with monasticism, I have come to believe that in one way or another we are all called to be monks in the world. I am not suggesting that you don a habit and fill your hours with fasting, prayer, and silence. I certainly am not recom-mending that you get stuck in the dogma-based religious rules and regulations that have been part of Western monasticism for cen-turies. But I am suggesting that to live a committed spiritual life in the world, you may have to live as a monk lives—with devotion to the spiritual side of things. More than that, I think monasticism contains many specific ideas and practices you will find useful as you build your own personal spirituality outside religion.

You may be surprised to learn that monastic life can be something separate and apart from religion. But this is the case, if you consider the basis for living in community as a monk. The purpose of living monasticism is to be free to explore the world of spirituality. To attain this freedom, monks give up three of life's most important preoccupations: ownership and the use of money, the pleasures of intimate relationships, and free will. The logic is that without having to deal with these time-consuming activities the monk has more time—all the time in the world— to be used for pursuit of a meaningful spiritual connection to the Source.

Living like a monk in the world can bring tremendous support to your personal brand of spirituality. Wayne Teasdale's book on this subject, *A Monk in the World: Cultivating a Spiritual Life,* presents the idea that we can all live by the spiritual values we formerly assigned only to professional spiritual seekers behind monastery walls. If we are to be complete human beings, we are all asked to surrender "greed, indifference, insensitivity, noise, confusion, pettiness, unease, tension, irreverence," and all the other negative qualities that diminish our spiritual aspirations.

Some time ago, a slogan circulated around the natural healing community, set forth I think by proponents of organically grown food: "Eat as if you have cancer." When I first heard the line, I was uncomfortable. I did not want to think of myself as having a disease. But the more I mulled it over, the more I liked the message. The admonition was that I should be avoiding junk foods and eating whole foods all the time, not just when my life was in danger. Fresh vegetables and fruits, uncontaminated meats and fish, whole grains, unrefined foods . . . I should be eating these things all the time, and by so doing I would avoid falling into serious disease.

When I suggest you consider living as a monk in the world, it is like that. Keeping a clear mind and a pure heart, staying open and free to explore spirituality in its myriad and magnificent forms, keeps you on a straight path back to the Source. Dwelling in the contaminated emotions and toxic thoughts of a carelessly lived life results in detours along the spiritual way— and often worse than detours, dead ends.

Earlier I said that I recovered three great spiritual values from my life as a monk and took them along on my search. They have stayed with me all these years, supporting and fostering my spiritual growth in ways I never imagined they would when I was still inside the monastic walls. When I was a monk, they were called by the names of the sacred vows: poverty, chastity, and obedience. I lived these values and experienced their transformative powers firsthand. Outside the monastery, I began to reframe them, going deeply into the true meaning and purpose of these vows. In time, I came to understand poverty as detachment, chastity as innocence, and obedience as responsibility.

The vow of poverty, taken by monks and nuns in all Catholic religious orders and by their counterparts in many other religious traditions, is about renunciation of ownership. A person who takes the vow of poverty makes a promise not to own any material thing, not even the clothes she is wearing and that seem to be a part of her. In monastic life, living poverty means that a person uses things without possessing them. Everything is owned in common (if that can be called ownership), but no one person owns any one thing.

When I first began to live the vow of poverty, it was not difficult at all. I was young and did not own anything of much value anyway. Really, everything in my life up to that point was consonant with the principle of poverty, since in my family as in most we all owned everything in common. Our house was not my father's or my mother's or mine, but the family's home. Our car was the family's car. Our clothes were ours, of course, but growing up in an Italian American extended family surrounded by a multitude of cousins, the order of the day was hand-me-down shirts, jackets, and coats. Some of what we wore might have been technically ours, but it was someone else's before, and likely would go to still another when we were finished with it.

In monastic life, as in family life at home, everything was provided for us—our meals, our clothes, the roof over our heads, an education, and medical care if we needed it. Our monastery was self-sufficient, so we had our own tailor shop, barber shop, maintenance shop, and infirmary. We did not use money, because there was no need to buy anything; we could not sell anything either, since we owned nothing individually.

Poverty sounds like "poor," but the reality of living the vow was far from what the word suggests. Poverty is often more an attitude than a practice of deprivation. We did not live the radical poverty of some religious orders, notably Mother Teresa's Missionaries of Charity. If Teresa's nuns are given a home to live in and conduct their work, they first empty it of furniture and rip out the carpeting, preferring to follow the letter of their vow of poverty. As monks of Holy Cross, we lived simply but in reasonable comfort. That is where the line falls. We did not go in need of anything, but we had by choice very few needs.

Detachment

Monastic poverty is not just about common ownership, or no ownership; it is about looking at what you value and placing a higher sense of worth on the intangible over the tangible, the spiritual over the material. The value of things is based on their usefulness, not their monetary worth. Under the vow of poverty, a car is something that gets you from one place to another; the make and model and year are totally irrelevant, as long as the car is a practical vehicle for transport. In fact, a car may be irrelevant if a monk's work takes him to a city that has public transportation. During eight years as a monk, I do not remember ever taking a taxi when a bus was available.

{ .. .. }

When, outside the walls, I began peeling away the outer skins of the monastic vow of poverty, I found at the core detachment. To look at something and not wish to possess it is detachment. It is to appreciate what we all agree are the good things in life but not hold on to them, to freely use them and be ready to surrender them the next moment. To enjoy, but to do so without clinging. Students of spiritual traditions recognize detachment as one of the essential components of the Eastern religions, above all Buddhism. But it is also a fundamental element in monasticism, whether Eastern or Western.

Probably the most obvious demonstration of detachment is around material things, including, in the first place, money. In a capitalist culture, living like a monk in the world is particularly difficult. Everywhere we turn, we are fed the idea that money makes the world go 'round. For most people, money—having it or not having it—is the definitive measure of success or failure.

This mind-set was encouraged early on in the development of modern capitalism by organized religion, most conspicuously Calvinism, which held in so many words that you could tell who was and who was not predestined to go to heaven by looking at a person's financial achievements. It may sound creepy, but that belief, inherited from our nation's Calvinist/Puritan founders, is as much a part of American culture as football, freeways, and shopping malls. The economic system we live under—and that now extends through multinational corporations and the pervasiveness of the entertainment media to virtually the entire world—promotes the value of money in and for itself.

Capitalism ("mercantilism," as it used to be called), means that you buy something somewhere, take it somewhere else, and sell it for a higher price. What results from the transaction is profit. Under the best of circumstances, a social interaction is at the heart of this commerce; people are really trading back and forth their individual energy and unique personality. In many parts of the world, haggling over the price of something in a market is a social convention, affording an opportunity for an affable exchange of homespun philosophies and observations on the human condition. Even when the price of something is absolute, buying and selling can be an occasion for an opening not only of the pocketbook but also of the heart. When I buy a dozen donuts directly from you, in other words, I get not just the donuts but also a part of you.

But there is a shadow side to capitalism. Over the years, we seem to have forgotten the human dimension in the act of commerce. Now, when I buy a dozen donuts in a supermarket, not knowing where they came from and not having a human face attached to them, I relate only to the donuts. When I identify myself with the donuts, the product, instead of our human interaction, I become a "consumer." The trouble with thinking of myself as a consumer is that I have to consume to live, and I have to consume more to live better. Calvinism and capitalism is a combustible mixture, creating an unnatural craving in us for obsessive self-improvement, so that we can be "saved." This is why money matters so much in our culture. The more money I have, the more material objects, or products, I can consume—giving me a platinum pass to eternity.

Like the shadow side of seeking, consuming snowballs as it goes along; it also tends to go on forever without reaching a level of satiety. When the Rolling Stones tell us in their signature song that they "can't get no satisfaction"—ever—they are holding the mirror up to our consumer culture, reminding us of the circular nature of the "never enough" way of thinking.

Detachment goes against the consumer mentality. Instead of getting caught up in the fear that you will never have enough, it asks you to end your addictive and ultimately futile search for the next bigger and better and newer thing. Detachment allows you to stop the inexorable drive to accumulate a huge quantity of material things you thought you needed to define yourself. Thinking of yourself as a consumer is a dead end, because it rests on the belief that you will never, ever have enough. Detaching yourself from things creates freedom. Imagine a man going out every day to buy and buy and buy, until his entire house is filled from floor to ceiling with things. Instead of reaching a point of "satisfaction," he has reached only a point of frustration, because he is unable to continue buying. Furthermore, there is no room at all to move around in. He has become a prisoner of his things, left sadly with only an increased craving to buy even more of them.

Living detachment means in the first place that you begin to entertain the idea of having enough—of everything. This requires diligence in our consumer culture, which works from the stance that a greater quantity of something is not just better but necessary. Moreover, as I said before, there is a spiritual dimension to contend with, an erroneous religious belief that God favors the wealthy, and if you possess a huge quantity of material things you are somehow morally superior.

The monk always asks the question the government asked its citizens during World War II, when gas was strictly rationed. In fact, it passed out little signs and asked drivers stick them on their automobile windshield: "Is this trip necessary?" What is really necessary to live in reasonable comfort? If, confronted by the barrage of advertising intent on creating false appetites, you ask yourself if this thing or that is necessary, you will be surprised to find that you can live without the newest and the biggest.

If you are reading this in your home, put the book down for a moment and look around the room. Is there anything you see that is not necessary? Is there an object that you purchased merely for the thrill of the purchase, something that does not perform a function for you? Naturally, I am not including an occasional painting or other art object, because these are necessary (within reason) to cultivate a sense of the transcendent in us and provide us with beauty, which the spirit needs as much as the body needs food. I am referring to things that do not serve us, and have never served us, and may never serve us, except as a way of supporting the consumer mindset in our belief system.

In recent years, simplicity has been emerging as a value for many people. There are even magazines that tell us how to live more simply. A bumper sticker you see from time to time says, "Live simply . . . so that others may simply live," applying the personal value of simplicity to a social and environmental setting. Detachment is like that. It teaches us to check in with ourselves moment to moment, to be aware of what we acquire and with what attitude we acquire it. Asking yourself *Is this necessary?* can bring focus to a issue that has been rendered purposely cloudy by merchandisers—impulse purchases, loss leaders, conspicuous consumption, and all the rest—and by their advance guard of advertisers.

When the monk practices detachment, the attitude is, "I can take this or leave it—it is all the same. If I have it, I appreciate and use it. If it is taken away, that's fine, too." In my teaching order, monks were regularly reassigned to different religious houses, and their schools, according to what particular instructional expertise was needed. For one semester, I might have been assigned to an upscale boarding school in the country, living in an estate donated by a rich benefactor. The next semester might have taken me to the inner city, where my precious few contemplative moments would be interrupted by the roar of passing commuter trains. I experienced both of those extremes in monastic life, and I can faithfully report to you that, living the vow of poverty (detachment), I was perfectly content in both those places, and in the several other houses to which I was assigned.

Detachment goes further. We have been looking at material things and thinking of objects "out there," but I suppose the most obvious material thing in our human lives is something much closer to us: our body. It is natural to be attached, since it is all we see when we look into a mirror. Our money-centered culture takes this illusion and runs with it, offering us standards of perfection that must be met if we are to be satisfied. Again, the consumer mentality, this time applied to our flesh and blood. The culture's attachment to the body shows up anywhere there is room for an advertisement. You are told your body is too fat, so you should take this pill or follow this diet. Your body is too old, so you should put on this cream or undergo this makeover. Your body is too sickly, so you should spread on this potion, or drink this concoction.

Obviously, we should take care of our body as the precious possession it is. We need to keep our body in the best of shape, maintain it, nourish it, exercise it, give it pleasure, rest it, and treat it with the utmost respect. But to go obsessively into these preoccupations is a spiritual dead end. When you are detached from your body, you cherish it for its usefulness and beauty, but you also realize that the you that is more than your body, that lives in several dimensions at once, is just passing through on the way to higher levels of spiritual awareness.

The challenge for us is to remember that we are spiritual beings making a human journey in the flesh, as Teilhard de Chardin suggested, and therefore we are more than our body. Still, detachment from thinking of ourselves as only our body is difficult, and it is not made easier by the culture of attachment that surrounds us.

Detachment

Earlier, I told you about one of my teachers, Hazel Archer. "Bundles" was Hazel's term for the distorted beliefs of other people we carry around through life as if they were our own truth. The only way to drop those bundles is to examine our core beliefs carefully and measure them against our own rock-bottom reality. Hazel also taught that we could have an attachment to ideas and inner pictures of how things ought to be, and they can get in the way of an authentic personal spirituality. Her example was seeing a man steal an apple. Immediately, in our mind, we cry "Thief!" By holding on to that definition, we have made the man a thief in our own mind, and we have built an invisible "thief" cage around him from which he may never be able to extricate himself. (The man may simply have forgotten to pay for the apple.) In a curious way, because of our mental attachment, he is now forced to be a thief, whether he wants to be or not.

"Withhold all judgment—be only a witness," Hazel used to say. When you withhold judgment, you are detached. You allow yourself the freedom to see a person or a situation clearly, without the overlays of what you may have implied from the appearance. She went even further, cautioning her students to avoid falling into the ironclad dualities of good and bad, right and wrong, success and failure. Who are we to make these judgments, anyway? If you were brought up in the Christian tradition, you will recognize this cautionary counsel as part of the compassionate philosophy of the teacher Jesus. Time after time, in the stories of his life, he is asked to make judgments on people and circumstances, and he refuses to do so. You will find the same admonition in the teachings of the Buddha and the other great spiritual teachers. "When you judge another, you do not define them," says Wayne Dyer, "you define yourself."

Are you attached to how you think about people? About national leaders, for instance—or closer to home, members of your family, people in your community, coworkers? Remember that when you render judgment on them, good or bad, right or wrong, you condemn them to act upon your judgment. It is a spiritual law. Are you stuck in your private ideology, your personal philosophy about how life works? You may want to look at those ideas to see why you are holding them so tightly, and whether in clutching them to yourself you are keeping away other, more constructive ways of thinking.

Attachment to ideas about how people should live their lives has been disastrous to our human species over the centuries. As one -ism is replaced by another, leaving a long trail of blood in its tracks, we lumber along unconsciously, forever looking for a new social or religious system to attach ourselves to. In the century just past, we slaughtered one hundred million of each other in trying to hang on to one ideology or another. Millions were put to death by their own governments simply because they did not conform to the right religion or the correct political position, or possess the good ethnic background of the perpetrators. Nazism, fascism, communism, bolshevism, socialism, Maoism, and all the rest—piles and piles and piles of dead parents, wives, husbands, brothers and sisters, lovers, wise grandparents, little children, all destroyed by butchers attached to someone's idea of how people should behave.

Just as you can become attached to mental constructs and pictures and find yourself forcing other people to adhere to them, you can have emotional attachments as well. In my experience, one of the most insidious emotional attachments centers on the sinister trinity of anger, resentment, and revenge. When I was growing up, my Italian American neighborhood fostered operatic expression of attachment to that volatile mix. Family members would "have words" with one another over some perceived slight and then would not speak to each other for years, throwing the rest of the extended family into chaos by compelling them to take sides. In many cases, the disputing parties took their feelings to the grave. Ironically, on Sundays everyone would be together in the local Catholic church, kneeling, standing, sitting, and listening to the parish priest preach a sermon on forgiveness.

So much of the advice we have received from the spiritual giants of the past is about letting go of anger, resentment, and feelings of revenge. Holding on to these lethal emotions, which always boomerang back to us, can have terrible consequences for everyone caught in the web of rage. Later, I am going to talk about another teacher of mine, Dr. Hazel Parcells, but I want to bring her in now, because of her beliefs about emotional attachments. Briefly, she was a pioneer nutritionist, a compassionate healer, and a professional wise woman. When a patient came to her with a terminal illness, she always went for the emotional attachment first.

Toward the end of her life, I went to live with Dr. Parcells, so I could learn her healing methods firsthand. One day, a woman arrived at her office with what I assumed was an unsolvable health problem. The woman had been diagnosed with liver cancer and told she had only a few months to live. She came to Dr. Parcells for a strict nutritional regime that might extend her life. But the doctor only asked her, "Is there someone you are angry with?" The woman immediately broke into tears and confessed that she and her sister had had a falling out years ago, and both had held on to their anger, which seemed to get deeper and more sour as the years passed. Dr. Parcells told her that she could do nothing for the woman until she reconciled with her sister. Anger, she explained, is a powerful living emotion; it runs all through the body, then lodges itself in the liver, where it can do fatal damage. The woman returned home and, without wasting a moment, phoned her sister. Working with a counselor, they were able to resolve their differences and dissolve their anger. Two years later, the last time I inquired, the woman was still very much alive, and the cancer that had been her death sentence was in remission.

Such is the potentially devastating effect of emotional attachment. Harboring toxic feelings negatively influences all the parts of our multidimensional selves—our body and mind and, perhaps most destructively, our spiritual life. No amount of medical attention can heal the body of someone who has become sick from holding on to hostility, sadness, jealousy, hatred, fear, apathy, shame, regret, or blame. No number of appeals to God or the angels and saints—the spiritual bypass—will heal the spirit if emotional attachments are not resolved at their own level. Give it up, let it go, detach, and watch the miracles unfold.

{ .. .. }

Finally, you can be attached to spiritual issues as much as to material things, your body, your thoughts, and your emotions. Spiritual attachment is about holding on to the unquestioned spirituality, or lack of it, that was handed to us as children. The imaginary pictures that fill our head and our heart—Old Man God sitting on a cloud and judging his creation, heaven with its choirs of angels, hell with its descending rings of fire and torment, purgatory, the hell-like waiting room in eternity, and all the rest. It is cleaving to so-called spiritual principles that have been put on our shoulders like Hazel Archer's belief bundles, even when we know deep in our heart they are no more than superstition. Spiritual attachment is seizing on a religious creed of someone else's devising, and clutching to it for dear life without asking questions, without exploring all its often irrational implications.

Nowhere is spiritual attachment more evident, I think, than in the musings of theology. All theological theories seem to have one thing in common: they are speculations about our origins and future, and our life in between, attributing to a divinity what we cannot otherwise explain. Over the centuries, the hypotheses of theologians became grander and more elaborate as our human curiosity and need to know ran ahead of our ability to figure things out from observation. Theological debates could get so convoluted—for instance, the qualities of the three "persons" who make up the Holy Trinity, Father, Son, and Holy Ghost. Quite learned people enjoined in endless deliberation and seemed to forget that the question at the heart of their argument was a fantasy to begin with. What can anyone say with certainty about a God someone made up, and someone else divided into three persons? It would be like you and me debating the exact shade of Little Red Riding Hood's little red riding hood. We could dismiss the theologians as irrelevant, and therefore not worth our time, except that down through the ages their attachment to spiritual invention caused the deaths of countless millions of us. They continue to do so in our time, calling it Jihad (holy war), Fatah (victory through holy struggle), or Operation Desert Storm—onward, Christian soldiers!

Spiritual attachment to sacred texts such as the Bible and the Qur'an is the basis for our present emergent fundamental-ism, which is running mindlessly rampant in all three of the monotheistic religions, causing all kinds of problems in the world. For most of us, taking a phrase from a book and giving it the power to influence our behaviors—and press for it to rule over the behavior of the rest of humanity—is simply nonsensi-cal. But just surf the television channels and you find ample evi-dence of these narrowly focused literalist attachments. This is not to say that you should not be inspired by spiritual writings in your search for your own path. To grab hold of certain chap-ters and verses, though, and make them the whole of your truth is to carry around an attachment that can sidetrack you on the way to personal connection with your Source.

A monk living the vow of poverty is detached from all these things, even from the past and the future. "Do not pursue the past; do not lose yourself in the future," the Buddha reminds us. "The past no longer is. The future has not yet come. Looking deeply at life as it is in the very here and now, you dwell in sta-bility and freedom."

{ .. .. }

Detachment is not the same as disengagement, indifference, or disconnection. As members of the human family, we are all invited to be active, participating collaborators in creating heaven on earth—for ourselves, for those in our closest orbit, and for all the living things who are passing through on this planet. Actually, when you live detachment you are more fully involved in life. You move into a blessed space where you are neither attached to nor repulsed from anything, able to see things more clearly, without fear, without judgment. You are a sacred witness. Dwelling in that place of "stability and freedom," you free yourself to soar to spiritual heights; you allow everyone else to do so as well.

CHAPTER EIGHT

innocence

> To see a world in a grain of sand,
> And a heaven in a wild flower:
> Hold infinity in the palm of your hand,
> And eternity in an hour.
> —WILLIAM BLAKE, "AUGURIES OF INNOCENCE"

LISTENING TO commentators on contemporary culture, you would think our modern obsession with sex is a recent arrival on history's stage. But a quick glance into the past will reveal that our ancestors, as far back as we can see, being no less human, had a similar fixation with sexual gratification, and it rose to a fever pitch of anxiety in some ancient civilizations.

Down millennia, the aura around the inexorable craving to procreate our species has been a tremendous mystery to us;

the intense, abandoned, ecstatic pleasure that accompanies it
but can run on its own engines, whether intending to reproduce
or not, has been even more of a mystery. Over the centuries, we
have touted and celebrated it, punished each other for expressing
it, denied it, hidden it from children, capitulated to it, and confessed it. We passed laws prohibiting it, overpowered and violated
each other with it, bought and sold it, built temples to it, blessed
it, and cursed it. None of our restless, self-conscious agitation
around sex has made it any easier to understand or know how
to deal with.

Perhaps something in our nature wants us to put the brakes
on our sexual urges. If this is so, we may have built our religions
around coercing us to be more responsible in that department.
Organized religions, intending to corral our senses and civilize
us, have always gone to the sex drive first, hoping to nip anar-
chistic human tendencies in the bud. Imposing restrictions
around sex in the name of God works, but only up to a point.
Eventually, the shadow side of sexual repression emerges, and we
hear about priests taking their altar boys to weekend cottages in
the woods and evangelists sneaking off to motels with their sec-
retaries. For the rest of us, there are the shadowy specters of
shame and guilt, pornography and prostitution, and a thor-
oughly unhealthy preoccupation.

{ .. .. }

On the eve of my leaving home to join the monastery, a week
after high school graduation, my best friend pulled me aside and
asked, "Are you absolutely sure you want to do this? Do you realize you would be giving up sex forever?" Without waiting for an

answer, he added a final question, trying to hold back a mounting sense of alarm: "Are you insane?" From the perspective of another eighteen-year-old, what I was about to do must have seemed irrational, and in a way it was; purposely surrendering a primary human urge and raging need is not something we do logically—or lightly. At the time, motivated by a strong call to service, full more of generosity of spirit and naiveté than reason perhaps, I made the step into monastic chastity.

The vow of chastity is just what you would imagine it to be: a promise to refrain from all sexual contact and sensual pleasure. It includes the obvious—no sex with others—and, maybe less obvious, no sex with oneself, no masturbating. Masturbation was a mortal sin for the Roman Catholic Church at the time, in any case, so this was already a prohibition for us young men at the peak of our sexual powers who went behind monastery walls then. A mortal sin, I should explain if you were not raised a Catholic, is a sin punishable by eternal damnation, meaning you go to hell after you die. I am not certain about the church's stand on masturbation today. Internet searches yield conflicting information: conservatives still say it is a sin with fatal consequences for the soul, and liberals say it is to be avoided for fear of falling into "self-love" (or they do not mention it).

Today, religious attitudes toward masturbation may seem more than merely old-fashioned. They may have been outright damaging to health, like telling people the only way they can get to heaven is to hold their breath. Once they take the next gulp of air, of course, the game is over and the devil comes up to claim the losers, and that would be all of us. Practicing Catholics may or may not still believe that masturbation is a crime against God

138

and nature, but many of the Christian sects preach strongly against "self-abuse," citing largely enigmatic passages from the Bible to support their position. They may be unaware of the oldest Egyptian religions' creation stories, antedating the Bible by many centuries, which begin with the god Amun going up to a high place to masturbate and bring forth the universe—an early version, perhaps, of the big bang theory.

Masturbation aside, monastic chastity is usually defined as refraining from sexual intercourse. The rationale is that a professionally chaste person will spend the time he ordinarily sets aside for lovemaking and its attendant dramas concentrating on spiritual matters. Chastity is similar, but not exactly the same as celibacy, which is required of all Catholic priests, and priests and ministers in some other religious traditions. Celibacy is simply the state of being unmarried. It is assumed, apparently, that being unmarried also means that a priest is refraining from sexual relations entirely. Other fine lines of distinction are drawn around these various proscriptions—examples of the convolutions accompanying religion and sex.

However, any way you look at it, and whatever you call it, for a person dedicated to a spiritual quest abstention from sex may have its place—next to occasional fasting, say, or retreating, or keeping silent for a period of time. We know from the Eastern religions that certain yogic practices are designed to withhold sexual expression in order to build the chi, or life energy force. Abstention sharpens the senses (I can report from my own monastic experience), producing at times a rapturous spiritual sensation that is like an orgasm, with the same strange time-stopping, out-of-body quality to it. When you read about some of the saints being caught up or transported during meditation, a sublimated orgasm is what is being described. Saint Teresa of Avila, the sixteenth century Carmelite reformer whom I mentioned earlier while discussing Saint John of the Cross, regularly went into these spiritual transportations. It is said that during her contemplations two novice nuns were assigned to stay at her side to hold her down when she started levitating—quite a feat, since Teresa was also said to be on the corpulent side. You would not know that from the exquisite Bernini sculpture of her "in ecstasy" in the church of Santa Maria della Vittoria in Rome, the very definition in marble of this elevated, euphoric state.

Living the vow of chastity in a monastic setting is actually less of a mystery than you might imagine. Something turns off inside. The mind goes to other things, the emotions quiet down, the body responds. What results from all this is a kind of wide-eyed innocence. You see it in the comportment of monks and nuns, particularly older ones, who have spent the better part of their lives abstaining from sexual relations. They have a childlike incorruptibility about them. Their faces are clear and pure, and their movements are light and airy. This is the quality of spirit I admired in monastic life and that I have tried to bring with me into my personal spirituality outside religion.

Innocence was our original human state, according to our Judeo-Christian-Islamic creation story and the creation myths of virtually all other world religious traditions. We came upon this garden planet in a pristine condition, a little less than the angels, pure of intention and chaste of heart. In time, we wanted to know what lay beyond the garden walls. When we found out it was a vast wasteland called "the knowledge of good and evil"—

the sense of separation—we were no longer the childlike creatures who wandered naked among the enchanted trees and flowers and waterfalls, naming the animals. From the creation of the
world out there to the world within, our personal creation story,
we come in as innocents as well, and as we mature we become
aware of the polarities.

Incorporating innocence in building our spiritual life means
going back to the garden, where life is not seen as a struggle
between good and evil but simply is—perfect and in no need of
improvement. To be innocent means adopting an attitude that
not only is nonjudgmental but goes the next step to believe
that people and situations are basically whole and complete just
they way they are. Innocence is about not having to manipulate,
not having a hidden agenda, ulterior motive, or cynical exit
strategy. Innocence is trusting.

Do you trust your body to do what it is supposed to do? Or
do you fear it, worry about it, mistrust it? Earlier I mentioned
Dr. Hazel Parcells, the pioneer nutritionist and spiritual teacher.
She observed that our body functions at a truly remarkable level
of efficiency when maintained in the simplest way possible: with
nutritious food, clean water, and light exercise. The innocence of
our body is a kind of miracle, when we think about it. It serves us
beautifully, without holding opinions, staying in excellent operating order and healing itself when necessary. All we have to do to
keep the body running perfectly is stay out of the way—trust it.

When we stop trusting our body, there is a loss of innocence
or an Edenic fall from grace. We surrender, mesmerized, to the
"inevitability" of chronic pain, terminal illness, decline, and
decay. Giving in to this insidious sense of separation we discov-

ered outside the garden, we regard our bodies as "other," and even (when we have dieted to desperation or worked out to exhaustion or had sagging skin lifted another time) as "enemy." Much of this mistrust of the body comes from our religious heritage, prodding us to self-improvement because we are fundamentally flawed, while at the same time disparaging the body as an instrument of sin. We tend to think of those poor souls who cut themselves on purpose, or wash their hands until the skin peels off, or pull their hair out, as mentally ill. But they are only more extreme expressions of the body's fall from innocence.

Mistrust of the body is not merely a physical problem; it affects all the parts of oneself and can stall progress in forging a meaningful connection to one's Source. If you find yourself slipping into an antagonistic, untrusting place with your body, you can recover that initial state of innocence by bringing awareness to your body's own native wisdom. One way to do that is to spend some time away from your usual daily routine to get fully back "into your body," to truly feel it and trust it.

{ .. .. }

Early one chilly autumn morning, I walked through shafts of sunlight illuminating pools of fallen golden aspen leaves, up a flagstone path, and entered a monastery. This was many years after I left my Catholic monastery in Indiana. This was a Zen Buddhist monastery high in the Jemez Mountains of northern New Mexico, about an hour's drive from Santa Fe. I had not gone there to live but to take a weeklong retreat.

One goes to a Zen monastery for *zazen,* the technique of meditation on which Zen practice is centered. The Buddha

himself sat in this kind of meditation when he received enlightenment under the Bodhi tree twenty-five hundred years ago.
Briefly, zazen is sitting in a certain position, back straight, as if
the top of your head is suspended by a string from above, and
concentrating on your breathing. That sounds fairly simple and
easy; it may be simple, but it is far from effortless, requiring as
it does complete and unwavering attention to posture, position,
and above all the movement of the breath in and out. Because it
brings together body, mind, and spirit (another word for breath
in Zen tradition), zazen is a holistic practice that can give you a
sense of being in harmony with everything in the world.

The little monastery in Jemez was a converted house, with
the barest of furnishings and amenities, as you would expect
when you think of the word Zen. While I was there, I wore a
plain, loose fitting cotton garment that looked like a bathrobe—
black, of course—and a pair of black slippers. I slept on the
floor, on an unpadded straw mat, with a single black wool
blanket over me. Meals were rice and some steamed vegetables,
served without salt or condiments. After eating in silence, I was
asked to clean the bowl I ate out of, dry it and the chopsticks
I used, and place them on the table under a napkin, making
everything ready for taking the next meal with the least number
of movements.

Zazen went on for most of the day, with generous breaks
for moving around in nature, which was splendid in the piñon-
flocked mountains and seemed to become even more magnificent as the days passed and my senses sharpened. The master
presided over zazen, both teacher and model of the ancient
process of centering and soul expansion. If I zoned out or dozed

off, the master tapped me on the shoulder with a long-handled tool, like a fly swatter, the exact name of which I forget—everything in Zen, it seems, has a special name. For instance, I sat on a *zafu*, a small round pillow, which is placed on a *zaniku* or *zabuton*, a large rectangular flat pillow. Zazen filled the days and the nights: three times during the week I was awakened at what I guessed was four in the morning for zazen, which included a *kinhim*—a glacially slow, mindful walking meditation through the moonlit monastery grounds.

The body of a person in deep zazen, or more correctly deep *samadhi*, is in a kind of suspended animation. When you are relaxed, you breathe about fifteen times a minute; in samadhi, you breathe two or three times a minute. With your mind completely at rest, your body goes into a profoundly relaxed state; it is in this state that the self-repairing body is mended at the cellular level with the least amount of interference. Ironically, although so much of Zen practice appears aimed at negating the body (care is taken, for example, in fluffing up the zafu pillow after zazen, to make it look as though you were never there), the sense of having a body and being in it is tremendously heightened. I took away from my Zen retreat a centeredness from which I could have direct experience of my body's presence and purpose—its innocence.

You do not have to go away to a Zen monastery to get back into your body, but taking time to be still and allowing your body to regenerate and revitalize itself is part of sound spiritual practice. You are probably already acquainted with a number of meditation techniques, perhaps yoga and other body-centered ways to relax and rest. Being at home in your body brings calm

144

and deliberation to your life at home and out in the world; it restores the sense of innocence and trust that is our native state and our birthright.

Living the vow of chastity, the monk practices innocence on many levels. When I started my monastery training, I was surprised to learn of something called "custody of the eyes." It means you do not look at every little thing that comes into the edge of your vision; you are not busy with what you choose to see. I realize this might seem like an extreme, even scrupulous spiritual practice to some. At first I could not understand what purpose it served and why I was asked to do it. But then, as I began to guard what I looked at, giving full attention to what I was seeing and avoiding darting to anything that turned up in my peripheral vision, a great feeling of composure came over me. Maybe this was part of what the Buddhists call mindfulness. You do not have to look at everything. You can choose what to look at, and when you do you will be using your eyes purposefully, seeing with concentration, intention, and awareness.

At the mental level, I believe innocence has a great deal to do with truthfulness. "False words are not only evil in themselves," Socrates told his students, "but they infect the soul with evil." As you build a strong and satisfying spiritual life for yourself, I encourage you to appreciate the beauty of truthfulness and entertain establishing it in all your dealings. We all are tempted to lie many times a day, whether by telling half-truths or outright untruths. Assuming you are not plagued by chronic lying (a symptom, often, of mental illness or at least personality imbalance), you have a choice of whether or not to tell the truth in a given situation. When you tell the truth, you are "blameless," as the *I Ching*, the Chinese book of wisdom, tells us. When you opt for untruth, for whatever reason—and the reasons can be many and compelling—you stray from the innocence of the mind.

"The truth hurts," goes the old saying. But nothing could be further from the truth. Actually, it is lying that can take a terrible toll on the health of body, mind, and spirit. Just the energy required for remembering a lie can sap even the liveliest intelligence. Think of a lie as a toxin in the mental body. It stays there festering, collecting around it many other untruthful contaminants, until it erupts as a serious character flaw. Lying is an obstacle to living a meaningful spiritual life. It hurts both the liar and the lied-to, unsuspecting souls who most often are trying to stay on their own spiritual path with integrity and depend on you to be equally committed to honesty. "Every violation of truth is not only a sort of suicide in the liar," Emerson says, "but is a stab at the health of human society."

A few years ago, I decided that I would not lie anymore. Lying had not been a huge part of my life up to then, but occasions came up where a well-placed lie seemed to be easier and better for all concerned than telling the truth. For instance: I have a solitary disposition. I enjoy staying at home, reading, working at the computer, renting a good film and watching it by myself or with one or two friends. If this sounds like the life of a monk, I assure you I was that way before I entered monastic life. There have been times in the past when, to protect my desire for solitude, I felt I had to lie. When the phone rang to invite me out, I invented stories to say why I could not accept. The ploy worked, so the stories became more elaborate and weightier. After a while, I possessed a sister I did not have, an imaginary elderly bed-bound aunt who needed my attention, a fictitious friend in the hospital whom I stayed up with all the night before, numberless pretend illnesses of my own, and so on.

The fantasy commitments I offered to friends eventually backfired. Once I was caught at the supermarket when I was supposed to be out of town. Another time, I was walking the dog in the park when I should have been at a birthday party for a cousin whom I had made up. These slip-ups ended in awkward explanations and embarrassing confessions. Covering for myself—lying—was interfering with my peace of mind. More than that, I began to understand that living in absolute integrity was essential to my spiritual life. Those red-faced encounters with people I had given false excuses to were a wake-up call for me. From then on I was determined to tell the simple truth, even joking about it: like Greta Garbo and Howard Hughes and J. D. Salinger, I just wanted to be alone. Grateful for my candor and relieved that I was not rejecting their companionship, my friends respected my need to be by myself much of the time. Something else happened when I stopped lying to protect my privacy, something seemingly paradoxical: I found myself accepting invitations to go out more. Lying had kept me in a kind of prison of my own making.

The other side of honesty is trust. If you are honest in all your dealings with people, they will come to trust you as a person of character, which is an integral part of walking a spiritual path. Think of the people in your life whom you truly trust, and you will see that they invariably have a deep spiritual connection.

Trust is one of the demonstrations of innocence. Living in trust is the first bridge to the brotherhood of humanity that has been eluding us down the centuries, but to which we aspire in earnest as spiritual beings seeking God on our own. "You must trust and believe in people, or life becomes impossible," says the nineteenth-century dramatist Anton Chekhov. He might have added that an authentic spiritual life becomes impossible as well.

Innocence of attitude is high on my list of qualities that make up a meaningful spiritual life. By this I mean the opposite of sarcasm, mockery, and cynicism. So much of our popular culture is grounded in ostensibly playful but nonetheless hurtful put-downs of other people. We are a culture of stand-up comics, or wannabe comics, often taking aim at the easy target to try to be funny. Surf the TV channels tonight and you will see what I am talking about. Sit-coms, with their biting edge of sarcasm and disrespect, are the worst. But this curious mind-set of contempt shows up in many other places, most blatantly in commercials, where parents are made to look like fools by their more perceptive children and men are reduced to ineffectual dunderheads by women. The romp of ridicule extends out from our entertainment into "meanstream" (if you will) culture via such vehicles as hate talk radio, vicious political and religious "debates," and the shouting headlines of the tabloid press.

This mean-spirited manner of discourse spills easily into our personal daily lives, becoming the way we relate to each other in our home, our workplace, and our community. I am not suggesting that you need to stop being cheerful in your exchange with others. Far from it. I am pointing to subtle threads of insolence and cruel cleverness that can weave their way in and around how you regard others and yourself and tangle into a knot that impedes your spiritual progress. Innocence is more temperate, but not less joyful. It asks us to be aware of the learned, automatic response that insults and denigrates people and situations in order to build ourselves up. Thinking pure (which is, after all, another word for chastity) creates a framework of acceptance in us that allows all who come into our orbit to feel welcomed and worthy.

Emotional innocence dwells in a place of no fear. When Chicken Little went around telling the other barnyard animals the sky was falling, he was coming from an inner sense of terror brought on by a single piece of evidence—bogus as it turned out—then blown all out of proportion. An acorn falling from an oak tree is not the same as the sky falling, but try telling that to someone accustomed to exaggerating and making a drama out of every trivial thing that comes into their experience. Exaggeration taken to its extreme can be a sign of serious mental and emotional problems, and the person usually pays for the inflated expression in the end. Chicken Little did, dragging with him into the fatal foxhole Henny Penny, Ducky Lucky, Turkey Lurkey, and the others who bought into his panic-motivated operatic scenario.

Exaggeration is mostly something we do when we are speaking, describing a person or an event. But there can be inner exaggeration also, as when we magnify something in our mind out of fear, anger, or other toxic feelings. Your friend borrows your car. The minute you close your door and hear the car drive off, you begin to imagine your friend backing out into traffic, colliding with a garbage truck, and you calling for an ambulance. Next you see your friend on a stretcher, a paramedic hold-

ing up an IV, flashing red lights, and so on, until you are sick
with grief . . . for nothing.

Anger is another emotion that tends to balloon in the mind
of an exaggerator. You leave the supermarket and count your
change, find it a dollar short, and in your mind pivot and return
to the store huffing and puffing, barging up to the checkout
woman, asking to see her supervisor, and on and on.

These inner upsets, leaving a long trail of pointless mental
debris behind them, get in the way of spiritual endeavor. The
unquiet mind is also an unquiet and distracted soul. I have run
across a number of thought-stopping techniques on my own
journey; some of them may be familiar to you. One of them is
the most literal imaginable. When you find yourself spiraling
downward on that self-destructive chain of mental pictures, just
visualize a big red stop sign. For me, that usually ends the domi-
nolike progression of negative thinking. Thought replacement
is another method to try. In this, when a negative thought arises
and threatens to spin out of control, you can replace it with
another, more rational thought ("I know this is an illusion, and
I am not going to give my mind over to it"). Image replacement
is still another way to quell unruly thoughts. In the examples I
have given, you could substitute for the imaginary auto accident
a rose in full bloom. For the supermarket encounter, envision
the face of a child or a favorite pet.

The best thought-stopper I have found is using a short, plain
phrase I made up. Sometimes we refer to it as an affirmation;
the Eastern religions might call it a mantra. "My life is sacred" or
"All life is beautiful" or some other phrase you create for yourself
can be both a thought-stopper and a reminder of, in this case,
the sacredness and beauty of all life. If you undertake such a

practice, you will find that your mantra comes up automatically when you are about to get aboard that unstoppable train of negative thoughts. When you come back to your true center, you are standing again in innocence.

In spiritual matters, I think innocence has much to do with avoiding dogma, doctrine, canon, theology. If you are seeking your own authentic spiritual path, organized religion's pat answers to the eternal questions are of no help at all. You do not need to be told that you were born defective and disconnected from your Source and that you have to spend the rest of your life trying to get saved through the agency of a priest, minister, or imam. You certainly do not need to muddle your thinking with the Holy Trinity, the virgin birth, the incarnation, the assumption, the immaculate conception, original sin, papal infallibility, transubstantiation, and the rest of the catalogue of fantasy tenets that make up the creed of various religions.

One of the great ironies of Christianity is its virtual disregard for the answer the teacher Jesus gave, more than once, when he was asked how to achieve a personal connection with the Source. "You must become as a little child," he replied. Little children cannot spout theological treatises, but they do know something about their own essential spiritual nature.

In 1836, Bronson Alcott published a fascinating book called *Conversations with Children on the Gospels.* Alcott is less known today than his famous daughter, Louisa May, the author of *Little Women,* but back then he was widely recognized and admired as an inspiring educator. He was a follower, along with Ralph Waldo Emerson and Henry David Thoreau, of Transcendentalism, which rejected all religious dogma and stressed the importance of intuition and subjective experience in communicating with the divine Source. At his Temple School in Boston, Alcott's primary method of teaching was to hold conversation with the children on what we would call the eternal questions—the origin of the world, the nature of being, the meaning of death, the purpose of our individual lives, and other topics related to their souls and to spirituality in general. He was astonished at their spontaneous, untutored replies.

> Alcott: Jesus said he was the son—the child of God. Are we also God's sons?
>
> William (age ten): Oh! before I was born—I think I was a part of God himself.
>
> Many others: So do I.
>
> Alcott: Who thinks his own spirit is the child of God? (All held up hands.)

Or this:

> "Can you say to yourself, 'I can remove this mountain'?" he asked the children one day. A six-year-old boy replied, "Yes, Mr. Alcott. The body is a mountain and the spirit says be moved and it is moved to another place. Mr. Alcott, we think too much about clay. We should think of spirit. I am spirit, not clay. I should think a mother would love her baby's spirit; and suppose it should die, that is only the spirit bursting away out of the body. It is alive, it is perfectly happy; I really do not know why people mourn when their friends die. I think it should be a matter of rejoicing. I cannot see why people mourn for

bodies." The first-grader was Josiah Quincy, who grew
up to become a mayor of Boston.

In some editions, Alcott's book of conversations with children
goes by another title: *How Like an Angel Came I Down.* It is the
first line of the poem "Wonder" by the seventeenth-century
British metaphysical poet and mystic Thomas Traherne. I
can imagine no words more eloquent to describe the spiritual
innocence required of all of us seeking our own way back to
our Source:

WONDER

by Thomas Traherne

How like an Angel came I down!
How bright are all things here!
When first among his Works I did appear
O how their Glory did me crown!
The World resembled his Eternitie,
In which my Soul did walk;
And ev'ry thing that I did see
Did with me talk.

. . . .

A Native Health and Innocence
Within my Bones did grow,
And while my God did all his Glories show
I felt a vigour in my Sense
That was all Spirit: I within did flow
With Seas of Life like Wine;
I nothing in the World did know
But 'twas Divine.

CHAPTER NINE

responsibility

You are responsible, forever, for what you have tamed. You are
responsible for your rose.
—Antoine de Saint-Exupéry, *The Little Prince*

EVERY MORNING after rising, meditation, Mass, and breakfast,
still in silence, the monks at our monastery would go to the bulletin board to read the daily schedule. This might sound mundane, but in a monastery the bulletin board is exceedingly
important because on it is posted the schedule for the day—an
hour-by-hour list of how the monks will fill the day, including
meal times and rest times. In monastic life, every day is by purpose nearly the same, so minute variations posted here were of
more than passing interest. Along with the bell that summoned
us to these various activities (monks call it *vox Dei*, the voice of
God), the schedule was considered almost sacred, detailing the

specific way our personal monastic practice would unfold in the moment.

There, among the times for spiritual reading, contemplation, and chanting the psalms, were our individual work assignments, called "obediences." The word referred to the vow of obedience, the promise to obey those who exercise authority in everything that pertains to the observance of the constitution of the order. In our case, "those who exercise authority" meant the local superior, who was the monastic head of the house, and above him the provincial superior, and above him the superior general of the Congregation of Holy Cross, our order. We did not take a vow to follow the dictates of our local bishop; it was assumed that in matters of faith we were bound to abide by church law, which was formulated in Rome by the pope and trickled down to us in rural Indiana. We were obligated to "forgo the independent exercise of our wills," in the words of our constitution, "in order to join with brothers in a common discernment of God's will. . . ." The key was to forgo, to allow the superior to make our decisions for us in all things.

The nature of a monk's obedience might be minor or major. A minor obedience would be an assignment as housekeeper, for instance, which means just what it implies: cleaning and overseeing repairs and other needs of the monastic house. Another might be comptroller, supervising all the expenditures of the monastery and doing the accounting. In a small house of ten monks or fewer, one was given several small obediences so that the same monk might be both housekeeper and comptroller, and in addition regulator, keeping the daily schedule. A major obedience would be an assignment to another monastic house with completely new duties. Whether the obedience is something as insignificant as cleaning a bathroom or considerable, like being appointed principal of one of the order's missionary schools in Africa, the attitude of the monk is expected to be unquestioning compliance. Over eight years of living the monastic rule, I never witnessed a single instance of one of the brothers refusing an obedience or even complaining about one. Once the vow was made, it seemed free will went into a kind of suspended state.

The conventional wisdom from the older monks was that in our youth poverty and chastity would be the challenging vows. What young man does not want to make and spend money, or explore his sexuality and sow his wild oats? Later in life, the really difficult vow would be obedience. Over the years, the desire to own property and accumulate a fortune would wane; the fires stoked by youthful sexual hormones would cool. We would become set in our ways, resistant to change, and less willing to comply with the demands of obedience. Still, even among the older monks—who you might think would have become more willful, not less so, with the passing years—breaches of the vow were simply unheard of.

{ .. .. }

There are enormous implications in giving up your personal free will to what you understand is the will of God. On the one hand, your entire life is safe and blameless. If you do not make any decision for yourself, you cannot be held accountable for the consequences of your actions. Life is something you float above, going this way and that steered by the hand of another. It is a passive way of living, in the sense that you are not really in charge of it; you are acting in your movie, but another person is directing. If something does not turn out well, this is no concern of yours, because someone else determined what you would do or not do. The burden of the choice of your actions is on their shoulders.

On the other hand, not having to make any decision whatsoever can leave a person indecisive and rather helpless. When I left monastic life, I had to confront this issue head-on. The first choice facing me outside the walls was the biggest, most urgent one: What should I do with the rest of my life? Years of allowing others to decide my life's direction left me poorly equipped to grapple with such an enormous question. I probably should have sought some professional help to get me onto firm ground, but at that time seeking counseling for life choices was not as common as it is today. I toughed it out for several months before I was able to choose a general direction, and even then I was not exactly embarking on a career path but merely enrolling in graduate school.

The shadow element in the vow of obedience appears when the monk begins to believe that, since he is making no decision, he has no responsibility. The constitution of my order anticipated such misinterpretation of the spirit of the vow and countered it with a specific statement of obligation: "Our vow of obedience itself obliges each of us take appropriate responsibility for the common good." It is exactly here that monastic obedience makes a valuable contribution to building a personal spiritual life for all of us. Responsibility—for the common good, certainly meaning others, but also responsibility for the common good of ourselves, the base of our spiritual operations.

Taking responsibility for yourself would seem to be the easiest thing imaginable. After all, you want what is best for yourself, so it must follow that you will do what is necessary and "appropriate," to use the term of the Holy Cross Constitution, to bring about your fullest expression and highest good, right? But you and I both know it does not work that way in the real world. The road to hell is paved with good intentions, as they say, and no intentions are better than the ones we hold on behalf of our own welfare. Because it is the key that unlocks so many spiritual doors, I consider responsibility to be an integral and indispensable component of a life that seeks a rich and rewarding connection with the Source. Practicing personal responsibility means you do not turn yourself over to someone else. You stand in your own power and, whatever the cost, tackle all the often difficult and demanding (and sometimes sublime) adult requirements of life by yourself.

{ .. .. }

In the infancy of our species, we invented religion and later many other fundamental institutions to make us more responsible. We created religion in particular to be a structure to restrain our curiously inhumane tendencies, binding us to act responsibly—not to kill each other, not to steal from each other, and so on—or suffer the penalties, which would be levied eternally at the divine court of the afterlife, and often at the prisons, torture chambers, and scaffolds of this life. In fact, the word *religion* comes from the Latin *religare,* to restrain or tie back—a way of restricting us from behaving like rogues on a bender. Living under the yoke of religion did not necessarily mean we stopped raping, pillaging, and strapping each other to the rack (frequently in the very name of religion), but imagine what crimes we might have committed *without* religion.

In the sky-God religions of Judaism, Christianity, and Islam, our rules of conduct were presented to us in a highly theatrical manner to underline their critical importance to humanity. Moses received them on Mt. Sinai literally from the hand of God, appearing as a lightning bolt and writing them in fire on stone tablets . . . but you already know this, having seen the movie. They are, of course, the Commandments, a list of thou-shalt-nots regulating human action, with an emphasis in tone on following them . . . or else. Depending on which source you consult and what belief you espouse, there are twenty-five, or nineteen, or ten of them. The Qur'an sidesteps their exact number and simply summarizes them with, "And We ordained laws for him in the tablets in all matters."

Growing up Catholic, I was taught Ten Commandments. Briefly, the first three of them pertain to God himself. Do not have "strange gods" before him, clearly a reference going back to a time when Jehovah, the God of the Hebrews, competed for worship with many other deities. Do not take God's name in vain, having to do with oaths, curses, and the like. Keep holy the Sabbath Day, the one day of the week given over to reflection on and gratitude to God.

The other seven commandments are about our relationship to each other. Honor our parents; do not kill each other; do not "commit adultery," which has borne so many meanings down the ages that it would take another book to plumb them. Do not steal or even "covet," which is to say lust after, the good reputations or possessions (including wives) of each other. Jesus, appearing on the scene thirteen hundred years after Moses, condensed all the commandments to a more compassionate (but just as forceful and apparently difficult to obey) three words: love one another. From his own Eastern tradition, the Buddha anticipated the commandment to love five hundred years earlier when he said, "Hatred does not cease by hatred, but only by love; this is the eternal rule."

You would think that by now we would have grown up and grown out of having to be told the basics of species survival—do not kill, in particular—because it is so obviously in our self-interest. But just when you start to believe we have made some progress since we hurled rocks at each other from the entrance of our caves, the morning paper arrives to dispel the illusion. Being told what to do and what not to do, even under the threat of eternal punishment, has worked but only up to a point. The time may be coming when we will have to leave our rebellious and antisocial moral adolescence, controlled by our God-parent, and step with both feet into a righteous adulthood where we stand, each of us, on ethical principles based on species brotherhood. Like the monk who has to turn the vow of obedience around to the idea of personal responsibility for it to be truly meaningful, we who are seeking God outside religion may have to find within ourselves a way to regulate our behavior on our own. This demands a personal code of ethics, an essential element in building a spiritual life.

The call to personal responsibility in how we relate to one another is not new to our postreligious sensibility. We have been looking for moral guidelines independent of religion at least as

far back as the time of the ancient Greeks. In the fifth century
B.C., the Sophists debated about how one should undertake personal responsibility in the same thorny matters as are taken up
in the Mosaic Law. Plato wrote about them in his dialogues featuring his teacher, Socrates. In the *Nicomachean Ethics,* Aristotle
wrote of the importance of behaving virtuously all the time by
cultivating good qualities of character, such as temperance, prudence, wisdom, justice, and courage, with the aim of *eudaimonia,* or success, in leading a fulfilling and happy life.

Aristotle's "virtue ethics" defined an entire system of morality that stressed the kind of person we should all try to be.
Roman philosophers evolved ethical theories from the assumption that we are born to act morally; ethics is part of human
nature. In the Middle Ages, Thomas Aquinas, Maimonides,
and others returned to the concept of natural law. During
the Enlightenment, with Thomas Hobbes, David Hume,
and Immanuel Kant, even more ethical systems abounded. In
Groundwork for the Metaphysics of Morals, Kant put forward his
"categorical imperative," the idea that there are absolute, unconditional requirements for how we are to behave, no matter the
circumstances. Jeremy Benthan, William Godwin, and John Stuart Mill disagreed and suggested that we must always act to
bring about "the greatest happiness for the greatest number."
Arthur Schopenhauer thought human existence was ultimately
evil and futile—a conclusion he came to, remarkably, after
inquiring into the Hindu sacred writings, the Upanishads, for
moral guidance. Friedrich Nietzsche built upon this pessimism,
and added that nothing mattered anyway, since everything was
relative. In the century just past, the Existentialists took it from

there and said that in an indifferent and confusing world we are all free to choose our actions and must accept the consequences.

All these musings on how we should act do not seem to have had the mighty effect of making us behave ourselves. In some ways we probably are more civilized, which is to say more educated, more hygienic, more refined, and now, with amazing new tools like telecommunications and the Internet, more aware of the world and our connection to each other. But much is left to do if we are to realize our potential to be truly human. I am thinking of the Yiddish word *mensch*, which literally means "man" or "human being" but is extended to define a person who possesses admirable characteristics, such as fortitude and firmness of purpose, a decent and responsible person.

Some modern thinkers, among them Michael Gazzaniga (*The Ethical Brain*), one of the founders of cognitive neuro-science, seem to be revisiting the notion of a natural law. They are suggesting that as the human brain evolves—and it is still evolving, according to the latest research, which contests the long-held belief that human evolution stopped around fifty thousand years ago—we are becoming more naturally responsi-ble. Our brain may have "moral circuits," dormant up to now or still embryonic and emerging, to take us up a grand step into an inviolable humanitarianism. It may be true, taking the long view, but we live here, now. Even if nature is working hard to help us realize our potential as responsible beings, the real work is still yours and mine.

Personal responsibility begins with what is closest to you, your body. We are growing up fast as a species, and learning that we may not have to give our body over to "professionals" to be maintained. Earlier I introduced you to Dr. Hazel Parcells. The content of her teaching and indeed her entire life spoke directly to the issue of personal responsibility. "If you want to be truly healthy," she used to say to her students, "you have to be willing to trade your wishbone for a backbone, and get to work."

She was born on a farm in southern Colorado in 1889 and died at home in the village of Sapello in northern New Mexico in 1996. You are doing the arithmetic. She lived into her 107th year and, until the last few weeks of her life, was robust in body and sharp as a pin mentally. For sixty years before she died, she did not need the services of a physician. She stayed healthy by taking responsibility for herself.

I met Dr. Parcells when she was 104 and was amazed at how sprightly and energetic she looked. She was a curly-topped red-head with bright, twinkling blue eyes and a wonderful laugh that made you want to laugh with her. I was told that she had full workdays, researching in her laboratory, conducting telephone consultations, and seeing clients (whom she called "students" to avoid any potential interference from snoopers bent on con-fronting her with practicing medicine without a license). She was perfectly qualified to practice healing in any case because she was a doctor of naturopathy and, in addition, held a doctor-ate in nutrition—one of the first ever awarded, I suspect.

She neither looked nor acted her age; in her mind she clearly thought she was much younger than she actually was. At the party celebrating her 102nd birthday, one of the guests was a retired banker, a white-haired gentleman of seventy-five. After the cake was cut and the ice cream passed around, she asked the man into her office for a private chat. "So you are a banker?" she said. "Yes, Ma'am," he replied. "Good. I would like you to help me draw up a ten-year plan for my investments." Momentarily stunned, the man said later he did not know whether to go along with the joke or open his briefcase and pull out his legal pads. Dr. Parcells, however, was perfectly serious.

After several visits, during which I took copious notes, I asked her if I could write a book about her and her healing techniques. She agreed and invited me to stay during the weekdays at her ranch home in Sapello, a small, idyllic settlement snuggled in the foothills of the Sangre de Cristo Mountains. Organizing the details of her remarkably long life and her methods for self-healing took six months. Reams of her early notations existed only on old onionskin pages; writing the book took another six months. *Live Better Longer* was published in 1997, the year after she died, but in her last months she was able to review the manuscript and approve the fine points of the material.

The life of Hazel Parcells is a perfect example of personal responsibility as a spiritual practice. During World War I she married and went with her husband, a soldier, to an army camp in Ohio, where sanitary conditions were inadequate in the extreme. That, and a particularly cold and wet winter, caused her to contract irreversible, degenerative tuberculosis. By 1931, single again and operating two beauty salons, she sank further into the clutches of her chronic illness. When she presented herself to a committee of doctors at the renowned Fitzsimmons Army Hospital in Denver, the verdict was grim: she had a collapsed lung, an enlarged heart, decreased kidney function, and other "terminal" ailments. Rather than try to treat her, the doctors suggested she take up residence in a wing of the hospital. Later she discovered that, though the wing was officially termed "convalescent," informally it was called "the death house"; patients might walk in the front door, but they were fated to be carried out the back.

In that moment, Hazel Parcells decided to live. She returned home and began a frantic search for what she could do on her own to restore her health. She went to the library and checked out everything she could find on the chemistry of foods. There was no science of nutrition at that time. She narrowed her inquiry to the healing qualities of certain minerals. Intuitively, she fixed on folic acid, which is abundant in spinach and other green leafy vegetables. "I ate spinach raw in salads and steamed and cooked in soups, and I drank spinach juice," she told me during one of our interviews. "I went through gunny sacks of spinach."

After a few weeks on her strict dietary regime, which included eggs and other simple proteins along with green vegetables, and an equally strict course of therapy in rest and relaxation, her condition turned around. In six months, she was well enough to return to work. A year after she had been diagnosed as terminal, she went back to Fitzsimmons for an examination. The doctors did not even recognize her as the same woman who had come before them the year before. Tests revealed that her heart was healthy again, her lungs were nearly normal, and her damaged kidney had regenerated itself. She was well.

In the years that followed, she became a passionate student of the chemistry of foods, racking up degrees, licenses, and certifications in the subject. Then she formulated a method for self-healing, based on her own experience, and began teaching it.

Simply stated, it was a program for staying healthy by eating healthy foods, therapeutic bathing, taking exercise, resting, and tending to the spiritual aspects of life by living in close cooperation with the natural world. She was an early and vocal critic of Big Agriculture, with its lethal arsenal of pesticides, fertilizers, and growth enhancers, which she said were destroying the life force of foods. "We are a culture that is overfed . . . and undernourished," she admonished. Only careful attention to what we are putting in our mouth and how we are treating the rest of our multidimensional self could keep us from becoming, in her words, "one of the walking dead."

Recent statistics on chronic ailments such as diabetes and heart disease, and conditions such as Alzheimer's and obesity (this last has spiked to include 66 percent of the American population), bear out Dr. Parcells's warnings and worst fears. Each year in the United States alone, more than 1.4 million people are diagnosed with cancer, and in spite of our "wars on cancer" and the aggressive interventions of Western medicine more than a third of that number die from it. At least 160,000 of these deaths will be related to diet. In fact, the vast majority of these disorders can be prevented by self-care, she insisted. She was born into a world without automobiles, a year before electricity came to her part of the country, when three-quarters of all Americans lived on farms, so her sensibilities were agrarian and her spirituality grounded in appreciation for the miraculous regenerative cycles of nature. That frame of reference, supported by her personal example of responsibility, is her great legacy to us, beset with crises of our own making in our technological, highly toxic, and in many ways highly irresponsible culture.

As I am writing this, the *New York Times* columnist Thomas
Friedman reports from Singapore, "There is something troublingly
self-indulgent and slothful about America today—something
that [Hurricane] Katrina highlighted and that people who live
in countries where the laws of gravity still apply really noticed.
It has rattled them—like watching a parent melt down." The
self-discipline required to take personal responsibility for our
lives has been eroding in our culture for some time. Over the
many decades of her long life, Dr. Parcells observed the erosion
firsthand, from handing our bodies over to the medical profession and saying "Heal me!" to giving our souls over to priests
and preachers and saying "Save me!" Naturally, there are times
when we absolutely need the attention of medical professionals.
Witnessing an auto accident on the freeway, you would not
phone for a naturopath or a yoga instructor. But so much of
what got us to the point of calling on them could have been
prevented by conscientiously taking better care of ourselves.
Likewise in spiritual matters, where a counselor or coach can be
quite helpful but a do-it-for-me, get-me-to-heaven attitude can
be ineffective (not to say disastrous) for finding a meaningful
spiritual path.

One of the most alarming developments in our culture in
recent decades is the emergence of pharmaceuticals to deal
with our emotional and mental health needs. In 1987, we spent
$1 billion on psychotropic drugs; by 2002, those expenditures
had risen to $23 billion annually. The ailments being treated
by these new fix-it-and-feel-good preparations are vast and various, with new (real or imagined) maladies being identified daily,
from schizophrenia and other serious disorders on one end of

the scale to mild depression and lack of focus on the other. How did we get ourselves into a position where we need to medicate merely to survive the normal process of living? Instead of popping a pill, which can offer only a temporary solution for a symptom, would it not be better to tackle the cause of the problem, if there is a problem, head-on and be done with it forever? If you are depressed, does it do any good to medicate yourself without bothering to find the origin of the depression?

{ .. .. }

Consider the role of personal responsibility in your emotional life as you build your bond with your Source. Many of us have become lax and lazy in this regard, and it has made us dependent on people and things outside ourselves for fulfilling our destiny. But if I am depending on you to take care of me, and you are depending on the next person, at some point we must all fall down like a house of cards. Nowhere is this dangerous dependence more evident, I think, than in the theater of relationships. The immature way to do relationship is to offer yourself to a partner as someone in need—ah, that word!—of completing or fixing. The mature way is to be present as a full and complete adult, capable of being responsible for yourself. If a relationship is based on mutual incomplete self-realization, low self-esteem, and neediness, it surely has to fail because two weaks can never make a strong, no matter how many relationship counselors are enlisted to the rescue. Taking responsibility for all your feelings is part of your spiritual aspiration.

Caring for our emotional body is as important as tending to the health of our physical body. People who live within a prison of anger, resentment, envy, greed, hatred, or other toxic emotions and put off dealing with them are irresponsible to both themselves and the objects of their venomous feelings. Hazel Parcells taught me that we are being called to do things differently. She said the time has come for us to take full responsibility for ourselves not only on the physical level but in the areas of our emotions, our mind, and our spiritual life too. As we come to more self-awareness as a species and therefore as individuals, we find that the old way, handing ourselves over to professionals for repair, does not work any longer. We must do it ourselves. Taking responsibility is truly living in obedience to the craving within us for the flowering of our fullest potential in all our many dimensions.

For the responsible person on a spiritual path, the sense of accountability the monk learns in true obedience extends to include the world outside. I believe you and I, singly and together as a culture, are answerable for our conduct. In *The Last Hours of Ancient Sunlight,* social critic Thom Hartmann informs us that every day forty-five thousand members of our human family, thirty-eight thousand of them children, die of starvation. Also each day 120 species that have taken millions of years to evolve become extinct; two hundred thousand acres of rainforest disappear; fifteen million tons of toxic waste are deposited into our atmosphere, our soil, and our water. In addition to these numbing indications of irresponsibility on a global level, we are recklessly using up the earth's natural resources at a shocking rate. In 2020, assuming we have not come to our senses, the *daily* demand for oil will be 120 million barrels. Such profligate usage will exhaust in twenty years the equivalent of all the oil humans have used in our entire history on the planet. Along with that gorging of petroleum will come attendant greenhouse gasses and perilous warming of the earth, and quickly upon that disastrous climate mutations and the rest of the calamitous story.

Are you and I responsible for the 842 million hungry people in the world who are fending off disease and clutching to life by the thinnest of threads at this very hour? Are you and I to be held accountable for the mindless destruction of our earthly home, for ruthless civil wars in Africa, for "ethnic cleansing" and wholesale genocide by unscrupulous governments? If we are, what can we possibly do about any of these things? Even Albert Schweitzer and Mother Teresa, with their full-time dedication, could touch only a few thousand of the millions who scream out for help every day; how many can we, in the midst of our own complex and demanding lives, reach and minister to? With what resources? For how long?

These questions go to the heart of the issue of personal responsibility. They are age-old questions, engaged diligently and seriously, as we can see by the amount of effort expended by the long line of brilliant and often inspired moral philosophers down the centuries. However, all their proposed answers may amount to only a partial solution.

"The way to do is to be," says Lao-Tzu, the Chinese philosopher and one of the founders of Taoism. The answer to the question of what you, the spiritual seeker, can do about the evils abroad in the world may be to live an upright personal life. The "way to do" planetary healing may be simply "to be" responsible for yourself and the people and things in your immediate circle. By being impeccably responsible in building your own spiritual life, as monks are invited to be by their vow of obedience, you model the magnificence of personal responsibility. In this way, you live at all times as you would want everyone in the world to live, in peace, with respect, in compassion, with forgiveness, in service, with generosity, in humility, with humanity, and the other noble virtues we have been pondering since the time of Aristotle. Imagine a world where everyone is living responsibly every minute of the day, all the time. The mind boggles; the heart exults.

In the end, you cannot be responsible for the whole human species; you can only be responsible for yourself. But as the sages and spiritual teachers have been reminding us for eons, taking full responsibility for your own body, mind, emotions, and spirit embraces the mystical healing of the entire planet. Since consciousness is one, if you have done it in yourself you have done it in all.

CHAPTER TEN

peak experience

Finite players play within boundaries; infinite players play with boundaries.

—James P. Carse, *Finite and Infinite Games*

After a respectful greeting, the letter began, "I agree, the work we are doing here would have specific application to the contemplative life you are living in your monastery. I am enclosing two information sheets I have compiled on the use of LSD to induce a mystical experience—or something as akin to it as my colleagues and I can tell." The writer went on to describe some of the experiments that had been done with psilocybin, a derivative of a certain species of mushroom, many of which he himself had directed. He closed with a promise to send me more research results about LSD and mysticism as they became available.

172

From this vantage point, the 1965 letter from Timothy Leary seems innocent beyond belief, even quaint, recalling what happened to Leary and to the world in the years since he wrote it. We continued corresponding back and forth half a dozen times, and then the letters with the annotated mimeographed sheets stopped; I read that he had been dismissed from Harvard, and shortly after that went off the deep end.

During my time in monastic life, I was fascinated with the idea of mystical flights. In the novitiate year, the first year of monastic training, I read as much as I could find on the subject in our small library. I read about mystical flights in the lives of the saints mainly, and in theology textbooks, which most often mentioned the transportation of mystics in discussions of over-heated spiritual preoccupations to be avoided. Later, as the rules relaxed a bit, I was able to read more widely and more deeply into the world of mystical experience. I discovered, among others, Simone Weil, the midtwentieth-century genius whose first mystical encounter came on reading George Herbert's poem "Love Bade Me Welcome While My Soul Drew Back." "It was during one of these recitations," Weil wrote in a letter to her spiritual counselor in May 1942, "that Christ himself came down and took possession of me. In this sudden possession of me by Christ, neither my senses nor my imagination had any part; I only felt in the midst of my suffering the presence of a love like that which one can read in the smile on a beloved face."

Weil's raptures were not unlike others I had read about, in the lives of Saints Teresa of Avila ("It is like feeling someone near one in a dark place"), Catherine of Sienna ("I became his bride in a mystical marriage"), Joan of Arc ("Blessed Michael the

Archangel spoke to me"), John of the Cross ("I went out from myself"), Margaret Mary Alacoque ("I felt suffused by the Divine Presence"), and Francis of Assisi ("I had the vision of a crucified seraph" just before he received the stigmata on his body). These experiences and others I read about are beyond the realm of ordinary consciousness; they are usually described as states of altered consciousness. In such a state, time seems to speed up or stop entirely, space expands or crunches in, and physical objects often appear vibrantly alive and full of color and light. It used to be thought that only the saints and people devoted to studying such phenomena (Thoreau, William James, Jung, Alice Bailey, and Jiddu Krishnamurti, to name a few) had mystical encounters. Now, however, we are discovering that they may be more commonplace: a national survey in 1987 revealed that a surprising 47 percent of Americans said they had had some type of mystical experience.

The accounts of people on LSD sounded to me similar to mystical experience. Thus my letters to Leary in trying to learn if authentic spiritual ecstasy could be induced by chemicals. By the mid-1960s, articles were surfacing in the underground press, and a year or two later in mainstream periodicals such as *Time* and *Newsweek* about the now-famous Good Friday 1962 experiment in the basement of Marsh Chapel at Harvard. Leary and his associate Richard Alpert, who would become Baba Ram Dass, conducted the experiment with Walter Pahnke, the study's author. The twenty participants were students of theology. Half the group took 30 milligrams of psilocybin, the other half received a placebo; all then went to a Good Friday service at the chapel. Interviewed afterward, those who took the psychedelic drug reported mystical experiences. It was an important experiment and might have marked the beginning of a significant investigation into the nature of mystical transportation, but as we all know LSD was soon declared an illegal substance, a lockdown on hallucinogens ensued, and all such scientific inquires came to an abrupt halt. Alpert went to India to continue probing the nature of mysticism; Leary defied the law and became a professional acid dropper and champion of psychedelic drugs for mind expansion.

Since I asked my first innocuous questions about psilocybin and mysticism, much has been discussed about the pros and cons of drug taking for any reason. For several years now, we have been fighting a war on drugs, with the U.S. government spending $1,200 per second in that ongoing and apparently futile combat. So it is difficult to get the topic of drugs and spirituality into perspective. As I said earlier, I have learned there are no shortcuts along the spiritual path, including taking drugs to try to force open the doors of perception. That said, I believe there is a place for what psychologist and philosopher Abraham Maslow called "the peak experience." I have found that building a spiritual life on our own, outside religion, can be immeasurably enhanced by these awareness icebreakers. They jar us out of our comfort zone, get us off the couch, and catapult us—ready or not—up to the next level of self-knowing. Under the best of circumstances, undertaken with courage and clarity of purpose, peak experience is of enormous value, especially to the spiritual seeker who may feel stalled in the process.

Maslow set out a human "hierarchy of needs" in his 1954 book *Motivation and Personality.* In it, he describes five needs we are born with and by which we are motivated to take certain actions. As you can imagine, the book had a tremendous impact on consumer culture, which was beginning to define itself during that period. The budding industry of commercial advertising and its cluster of conduits—entertainment radio, general-interest magazines, wide-circulation newspapers, the nascent medium of television—were spellbound by the implications of Maslow's work. If you knew what people needed and wanted, you could sell them anything. The needs were biological and psychological (air, food, sleep, and sex); safety, as in protection from the elements and security; a sense of belonging and love, such as work group, family, and relationships; and esteem (self-esteem, achievement, status, prestige, and dominance). You can see why Madison Avenue would have perked up at the list of these behavior motivators. Needing a car to go from one place to another is one thing; needing a car to increase self-esteem and to bestow status is quite another. Economist John Kenneth Galbraith, looking nervously at advertising's use of psychology for manipulation, said it was upsetting the classical balance of supply and demand, creating a high level of demand for products that consumers never knew they wanted, much less needed.

The fifth need is a bit different and gets into an area of being human that we have only recently begun to think through: self-actualization, as in realizing personal potential, self-fulfillment, seeking personal growth, and peak experience. Yes, Maslow believed we all need peak experience to fulfill ourselves. He described it as a sudden feeling of intense happiness and well-being, and possibly awareness of ultimate truth and the unity of all things. Accompanying these experiences is a heightened sense of control over the body and emotions, and a wider sense of awareness. Sometimes they can come on seemingly spontaneously, triggered by nothing in particular. At other times, they can flame up into us while we are watching a glorious sunset or a full moon, or looking at a leaf or a flower. They can be induced, as well, by mood-altering or mind-altering substances or by out-of-the-ordinary physical changes, like fasting, sleep deprivation, sexual abstinence, or the endorphin rush that follows strenuous exercise.

My first peak experience, at least the first I can remember, took place when I was eight—I spoke about it earlier. It came on out of nowhere, while I was running around playing with other children, a feeling of serenity and well-being so intense that it nearly put me in a swoon. The sensation was radiant and profound, delivered with such impact, that I recall everything about it to this day. You no doubt have several of these experiences in your personal history, and one or two that are so memorable they are the first images that flashed through your mind as you began to read this section. You will have had some peak experiences you brought on purposely, whether it was experimenting with holding your breath as a child or going into riskier areas with mood and mind alterations as an adult.

Peak experience is important to building a spiritual life, I believe, because it gives us a brief glimpse of what we are striving for in the first place. We began our spiritual search out of a craving to know where we came from, who we truly are, and where we are going. These extraordinary glimpses hold part of the answer to the eternal questions. They stop us in our tracks, remove us for a few moments from the mundane and largely unconscious way we move through life (the "plateau," another Maslow term), and remind us about living in full awareness of our multidimensional nature. They are windows that open a crack to let in the sights and sounds of "real" reality, confirming that union with our divine Source is possible.

One recent peak experience came to me as a complete surprise, during an event I was facilitating as a peak experience for other people. A little background: with two colleagues, I lead guided retreats for people seeking life path clarity. Several times during the year, we invite a shaman to facilitate a retreat with us. Our shaman is Eduardo Morales, from Tepoztlan, Mexico, south of Mexico City. The first time I visited Tepoztlan many years ago, it was described to me as *un nido de curanderos,* a nest of healers. I thought the choice of the word *nest* was peculiar, but by the second day of my stay I began to understand the reference; magic goes on there. Tepoztlan is sometimes called "the sacred valley" for its long history of metaphysical associations. It is the legendary birthplace of Quetzalcóatl, the plumed serpent of ancient Mesoamerican mythology, the principal deity of the Aztec pantheon. The supernatural focus of the town was, and by some accounts still is, the small pyramid atop Mt. Tepozteco, reached by a gruelingly long set of narrow steps hewn into the side of the mountain. The pyramid is a temple to Tepoztecatl the god of *pulque,* a euphoric alcoholic beverage made from the sap of the cactuslike agave plant. Pulque is still used in some indigenous rituals in Mexico, but mostly you find it in village back streets, in special bars, called *pulquerías,* where women are not allowed and goodness knows what psychedelic visions float around behind the saloon-style louvered doors.

Like all the residents of Tepoztlan, Eduardo is fiercely proud of his spectacularly beautiful town and its mystical heritage. He carries the spirit of that place with him wherever he goes, and he has gone far and wide, to Canada (adding French to English and his native Spanish), Europe, Latin America, and the United States, where he regularly gives workshops in shamanism. He does not use pulque, *ayawasca,* or any other hallucinogen in his work, which is remarkable and deeply transforming.

The role of the shaman is prehistoric. He (occasionally she) is a member of the tribe singled out to go to "the other side" to bring back information the tribe needs in order to live in balance. This person goes by the name of *shaman* in Native American tradition (the word itself is derived from the Tungas language of Siberia, indicating, perhaps, the primordial origin of the office) and by other names in other cultures. Eduardo does not often call himself a shaman, but this is what he is. The shaman's task is critical, for without him the tribe would not have access to the great mysteries and would fall into a pit of ignorance, ill health, and immorality. They would revert to their primitive animal nature. The contemporary shaman continues to be called on by the tribe, whether on a humble Indian reservation or in a busy metropolis, especially when a seeker needs healing with a spiritual dimension.

Eduardo told me about a recent case where he was flown to Italy to try to help a four-month-old baby boy named Nicolas, who was hovering near death. His distraught parents had consulted every imaginable medical specialist, to no avail. When Eduardo got to the hospital, Nicolas was in critical condition, trying to adapt to a second liver transplant. After several days of communing with the boy's spirit, he discovered on "the other side" the answer to the problem: two spirits were contending for the same body.

The liver that Nicolas received belonged to a thirty-two-year-old woman who had died in a motorcycle accident, a fact he pieced together from the scantest of evidence since it was hospital policy not to reveal the name or death circumstances of the organ donor. Now, a conflict had arisen between the spirit of the boy and the spirit of the liver's original owner. The woman's spirit was surprised to find that she was still alive in a physical body and was confused. Assuming she was continuing to live in the flesh, she naturally wanted to claim the baby's body as her own. In the confusion, she was dragging the body of Nicolas into a premature physical death. Eduardo began to mediate between the two spirits. The challenge was to try to get their spirits to work together for the benefit of each other. If the woman's spirit would agree to depart and go on with her life on the spiritual plane, Nicolas would be able to live fully in his own body. On the boy's part, he would have to agree to take on responsibility for the organ by becoming its new owner, allowing the first owner to depart. Communicating with the spirits, Eduardo's attitude was, "Let's work together to bring about the best for both of you."

From that day, Nicolas began to regain his health. Two months later, he was well enough to leave the hospital. His grateful parents took him home, where he continued to improve. As I write this, Nicolas is a healthy, energetic, curious, normal two-year-old. Some on the team of doctors said it was a fluke the liver was not rejected; others said it was a miracle. For Eduardo, it was all in a shamanic day's work.

But back to my own surprise peak experience. In our retreat, we were working with a group of eighteen people. The center-piece of the weeklong program was a rebirthing at night at one of the local thermal springs. Not all shamans specialize in rebirthing, but Eduardo does and has for fifteen years. Rebirthing, induced by certain breathing techniques in a special setting, takes people back to their original birth, this time with awareness and the opportunity to recall all the physical, mental, emotional, and spiritual conditions of those unique first few moments of life. Knowing more about what attended their birth, they are able to identify and work with patterns of behavior that have been with them since their entrance onto the human stage.

Rebirthing began in the 1960s, around the same time as the early experiments with psilocybin and other mind-altering sub-stances. Recently, it has been going under the name of holotropic breathwork or applied breathwork, because the peak experience is brought on by certain breathing techniques in a relaxed state. Leonard Orr began working with the method first, and then it was taken up by psychotherapist Stanislav Grof, dubbed in pro-fessional quarters "the godfather of LSD," a title he acquired pioneering the psychotherapeutic uses of the drug in Prague as early as 1960. There are deep breaths interspersed with a series of short, sharp breaths, then deep breaths again, and so on in a prescribed round. The point of the breathing practice is to let go of limiting thoughts and feelings, permitting higher awareness to emerge. In time, sometimes a minute or two after one begins the breathing exercise, something begins to happen.

As I said, I was at the hot springs that night to help Eduardo and my colleagues facilitate the rebirthing of our retreatants. I had facilitated others' journeys many times before in previous retreats. This time, overtaken by the immensity of the moment perhaps, or maybe simply because it was my turn to have the full experience, I became a baby again.

Floating there in the warm water, I began to feel an intense, tingling rush of energy throughout my body and a tremendous sense of inner focus. The feeling was not entirely unpleasant, but since I was not expecting it to happen it was startling. I allowed one part of my brain to remain stunned and embarrassed—I was supposed to be one of the teachers, after all—and put it away in a kind of mental drawer so I could fully experience what was unfolding. Though I was completely conscious, I was going somewhere deep inside myself, bringing up memories from my birth. I felt my face constricting on the sides, becoming long and narrow, and my hands curling up into my chest in a fetal position, fingers stuck together and pointed toward my body. Slowly, I made my way in my imagination down the birth canal and out into the world.

Time ceases to exist during a soul experience like this, so I do not have a good grasp of how long my actual birth reenactment went on. When we got into the water, the late afternoon light was still with us. By the time I was "born" and staring at my hands, which I did not recognize as my own for what seemed like half an hour, it was dark and the stars had come out. I took away from the spontaneous rebirth a seemingly endless string of insights, but two of them were so powerful that a chill runs through me now in writing about them. First, as I was beginning to rise out of the cellular memory of my original birth and realizing that I was back on earth again, I felt an enormous disappointment, a letdown of cosmic proportions. I heard myself saying over and over, "No, no, not again, no!" Disillusioned and frustrated, I started to weep. I was an infant, crying myself into the world. My tears mingled with the soothing waters of the natural springs, ancient waters that had been waiting in the bowels of the planet for untold eons. "I can't, I just can't," I said, exhausted.

Eduardo, who had been looking on, touched me lightly on the shoulder and whispered a few reassuring words. Then something shifted and, still staring at the palms of the two strange hands before me—my hands—I sensed the glow of a great light somewhere deep within me and felt myself surrender to its insistent warm embrace. Love, love all through me, and with it unconditional acceptance, joy, unutterable gratitude. Words cannot get to the feeling. I felt transported, floating on the surface of an overwhelming parental love, which extended outward to embrace all living things, and myself giving love for love. For a long time, I luxuriated in the marvelous sensation, the consolation for having agreed to return once again to this planet of soul lessons to live the human journey and in some way to serve.

Rebirthing offers numerous opportunities to enrich your spiritual life, while at the same time correcting long-standing emotional, mental, and physical problems. It can help to answer the puzzling question, Why are you the way you are? The circumstances surrounding your birth are significant. Knowing them can bring you to an understanding of deeply engrained patterns in your present life. Were you a late arrival? If so, you may find that you are always late showing up in your daily life, or you may feel that you are constantly trying to catch up, whether the task is as simple as dusting the living room or as complex as cramming for the bar exam. Were you early? You may feel driven to be a high achiever to the point where it interferes with normal living, or you may be so impatient that your intolerance with other people's "unendurable" behavior borders on neurosis.

During your mother's pregnancy, were she and your father together? Did they want you? Was your mother young and afraid? Was your father worried that he would not be able to provide for his family once you arrived? Did your mother desperately want to give birth to a boy but you knew you were a girl, and therefore a disappointment before you even breathed your first breath? Did your mother think of aborting you during the pregnancy? Did your father beat your mother? All these things, and more, including what your parents were thinking and dreaming about during your incubation, exerted a fundamental influence on who you are and why you live your life the way you do. Eduardo told me that the newborn baby carries in its cells the memories of traumas inherited from not only mother and father but grandparents as well. We are, after all, the result in flesh and blood of a long, long line of flesh and blood that goes back to the first hominoids, and further back to their progenitors.

Birth and death are the special theaters for shamanic activity. The shaman acts as a guide for those two irreversible brackets of human existence, helping the rest of us to the next step. Following an ageless tradition, he goes into the underworld of the human unconscious to retrieve knowledge we never had or forgot we had. Then he journeys back to the upper world, our world, with the vital trophy. It is an arduous task. During one

of the subsequent rebirthings I helped to facilitate, Eduardo said
he needed to stay behind to bless the spring waters and return
them to their undisturbed state, but when we went to look for
him after a while we could not find him. He seemed to have dis-
appeared. Then, just as suddenly, he reappeared and went on
with his work. Had he shape-shifted to the owl whose mournful
whoo-whoo had been drifting in on the night air? If so, did he
do it to recharge his energy, so generously spent negotiating
between two worlds?

⟩ .. .. ⟨

Toward the end of my first year in monastic life, the year of training, I experienced something I have never told anyone about—
not because I was embarrassed or otherwise uncomfortable
about sharing it, but because I do not know if it really happened.
Near our monastery lay a lake, and in the middle of the lake there
was a small island. Two or three times during the summer, we
were allowed to shed our black habits for an afternoon, dress
in mufti and go out in boats to the island for a picnic. This was
our year of silence, so all the preparations for the outing and the
crossing itself were done without speaking. On the way to the
island, rowing alongside one of the other brothers, I began to
feel uncommonly peaceful and serene. As we docked at the
island and moved the food to a cluster of picnic tables, my
mood deepened and I could sense my attention ebbing from
what I was doing and attaching itself to something else.

Long shafts of sunlight were falling through the tall oaks
and maples. With heightened senses, I could hear the buzzing of
flies, gnats, bees, insects of all kinds, and birds and the cracking

of twigs and crispy leaves falling to the ground and the lapping of water on the thin shore of the island. Then I saw myself sitting at one of the picnic tables, blessing my food with the others, slowly eating. I watched as I picked up a glass of lemonade and drank from it. I observed myself lifting a forkful of food to my mouth, chewing it, sipping from my glass. After that, all I can remember is feeling so completely relaxed that it was as if I had gone outside my body entirely. Caught in that long moment, I felt held, caressed, cradled. In this strange and wonderful place of perfect well-being, I had no concerns whatever. I did not have to do anything to be me. I did not have to move or think or even breathe to stay alive.

The mystics report (to the extent they can verbalize it) a sense of being in a kind of suspended animation where there is nothing but breathtaking wonder. Out of the vocabulary of their religious milieu, the saints call it being caught up and held in the arms of God or Jesus, or being arrested in ecstasy at beholding the face of the Virgin Mary or an angel. I am not sure what came over me on that long-ago afternoon, except that I knew suddenly, unequivocally, that I was an eternal entity. I had always been and I always would be, and my true nature and condition is bliss, pure and simple. Whatever a peak experience is supposed to furnish in Maslow's hierarchy of needs, surely the profound recognition of our essential spiritual identity must be a large part of it. Experience is the key, because it is one thing to study, research, learn, know in your head, but something else entirely to experience.

On the island, gradually, the blissful state the yogis call the seventh heaven, the last frontier between the Creator and the created, left me and I felt myself localize into this body, felt my limbs, rubbed my eyes, breathed. But I do not remember the rest of the afternoon and evening, which must have included leaving the island, rowing back across the lake, and returning to the monastery grounds. As I said earlier, I am unclear about the whole episode. I cannot say confidently that there ever was a lake, or in the middle of the lake an island, or on the island a picnic of monks. I might expect not to remember every detail of something that purportedly happened nearly half a century ago, but even five years, two years, afterward I had the same misgivings. In a way, it does not matter. William James, the father of American psychology and author of *The Varieties of Religious Experience* (1902), tells us that the first characteristic of mystical experience is ineffability—it cannot be explained. It is a "state of feeling." Those caught otherworldly moments are forever with me and sometimes seem like the *real* real world glimpsed through a crack in the window. What remains is the memory of the experience, and that is more than enough.

Twenty-five years after the Good Friday Marsh Chapel Experiment with LSD in the early 1960s, a follow-up study was attempted. By then Walter Pahnke had been dead for a number of years and most of his research notes were lost, but Rick Doblin, a psychology student at New College in Sarasota, was able to conduct interviews with almost all of the participants. He published the results in the *Journal of Transpersonal Psychology*. Everyone who had been administered the drug in that sacramental setting felt they had a genuine mystical experience and that the "clear viewing of some ultimate level of reality . . . had a long-term positive impact on their lives." Doblin later summed up his findings to a newspaper reporter: "The primary feeling of unity from their drug trip led many of them to a feeling of compassion for oppressed minorities and the environment." Their mystical peak experience did not end with personal growth. Going deep inside for these subjects impelled them, years later, to go outside of themselves and embrace the world. The same could be said of most of the traditional mystics I studied. St. Francis's exquisite altruism endures down the centuries in his universal paradigm of simple living. Teilhard's high humanitarianism is embedded in his sweeping cosmic vision, urging us to reach for the stars.

One day at the film school in Santa Fe, I returned to my office from teaching a class and was handed a phone message. A woman named Joanna Leary wanted to have lunch with me. Could this have been Joanna Harcourt Smith, internationally known as Mrs. Timothy Leary, whom the press of the early 1970s nicknamed "the Acid Queen"? When I called her back, I discovered she was indeed the same Joanna. Over lunch, she told me she was interested in hiring some of my film students to make a video of a presentation she was evolving on sobriety as a personal spiritual practice.

In the weeks that followed, we became friends and she shared some of her memories of her life with Leary, a few of them incandescent, others wrenching. When they met she was twenty-six, the daughter of a British aristocrat who was a spy during World War II; Leary was fifty-three. At the time, the charismatic high priest of LSD was a fugitive from the law, in hiding in Algeria and Switzerland. Joanna became his wife and they moved from place to place, ending up in Afghanistan, where they were captured by U.S. government agents and taken to California. Leary went to prison for three and a half years on a ludicrous drug charge (they found 0.01 grams of marijuana on him) but actually to be made an example of, while she worked tirelessly to get him released. When I asked her how often they took LSD during their time together, she looked at me as if I had not been listening. "Every day," she said.

Today Joanna is an author and activist working in the new field of deep ecology, a mystical approach to environmental science that espouses rethinking society's values to sustain life on earth. She follows a personal spiritual path of great substance, devoted to bringing others into alignment with their own spiritual aspirations. Helping people with addictions get sober and stay that way, which was one of her passionate concerns when I came to know her, has evolved into the much wider cause of guiding people toward planetary awareness and responsibility. In her own life, certainly an extreme and premier example, she confirms the accounts of the Marsh Chapel participants, whose mystical experience led to "a feeling of compassion for oppressed minorities and the environment." Joanna told an interviewer recently that she owes her zeal for planetary healing to "the spiritual intelligence and the reverence for life I experienced during the psychedelic experience."

The ultimate purpose of the peak experience may be to take us outside of ourselves. If Maslow was right, then going out to others must be one of our indisputable human needs. What we see through the crack in the window may be the spiritual truth that we are indeed one with all, a vision that can elicit in us only an all-encompassing compassion.

PART FOUR

being

CHAPTER ELEVEN

service

We work our whole lives building our lives, and to what end?
I believe it is, finally, to give it away to others. By this means,
our life becomes a seed. Planted in the imagination of one who is
ready to receive it, harbor it, and nourish it, the seed becomes
the life of the future.
—HAZEL PARCELLS, IN *LIVE BETTER LONGER,*
BY JOSEPH DISPENZA

ON DECEMBER 24, 1968, something occurred that could turn out
to be as dramatic and decisive for the evolution of human consciousness as the return of Christopher Columbus to Spain on
January 16, 1493. The *Apollo 8* spacecraft, circumnavigating the
moon, took a picture of Earth rising five degrees above the lunar
horizon. On the earth, the "sunset" shadow crosses Africa.
The South Pole appears as a white area near the left end of the

shadow. Clouds hide North America and South America. There was our whole planet, set against space's vast black backdrop. For the first time ever, we saw with our own eyes the entirety of our human home. Nine years later, pictures were beamed down to us from near space showing both the earth and the moon hanging brightly in the dark heavens. Then in May 2003, we received photos from NASA's Mars Global Surveyor showing the earth and the moon from the surface of Mars, thirty-six million miles away.

Taken together, these and other spectacular photographs from space are giving us a radically new idea of where we are. We used to think we were living on a giant globe divided by barriers of politics, culture, race, ideology, language, topography, and religious belief, but these pictures—objective evidence from outside ourselves—show no barriers at all. From out there, our home planet is a seamless heavenly body. We thought our world was immense and unfathomable, but here it is, looking quite finite and therefore fathomable given the time, and not that immense either; staring at a photograph from *Voyager 1*, astronomer Carl Sagan murmured reverently, "A pale blue dot."

As those images sink into our collective consciousness, we are gradually coming to a new awareness of ourselves as islanders afloat in space, with islanders' responsibilities, part of an undivided, planetwide human family. However, the promise of that awareness may be only a hint of the new way we will be seeing our world and ourselves in the next few years. If the sixteenth-century voyages of discovery gave us a new cosmology, perhaps the impact of pictures of our planet from space will give us the opportunity to construct a new ethics and metaphysics as well.

"Think of the rivers of blood spilled by all those generals and emperors so that in glory and in triumph they could become the momentary masters of a fraction of a dot," Carl Sagan wrote later. "Think of the endless cruelties visited by the inhabitants of one corner of the dot on scarcely distinguishable inhabitants of some other corner of the dot." Now that we can see where we are and that where we are is a whole and living thing, we might finally be in reach of understanding the absurdity and futility of butchering one another over arbitrary lines drawn in the sand. Ironic that the arresting icon of planetary wholeness should come to us near the end of a century of unprecedented division, what many historians are calling the bloodiest of centuries, almost like an exclamation mark shocking us out of our self-destructive species childhood.

{ .. .. }

Gazing mesmerized at the tiny, lovely blue marble rolling on the placid black sea of space, we hear the echoes of the timeless questions rushing back to us: Who are we? Where did we come from? Where are we going? What is the sense of it all? Behind these macrocosmic questions is the great puzzle of our individual existence, its purpose, its origin, and its future. In our species infancy, to pry open these grand enigmas we remembered a connection to the Source of all life and, believing ourselves separate from it, set about restoring the vital bond. Religion was one way we went about the task of reconnection. Now we are finding that religion as we created it has not only not connected us with our Source (it cannot, really, because of its inherent premise that we are unworthy to approach our Source) but has tragically disconnected us one from another.

The failure of organized religion to bring us connection has ignited in a growing number of us the urge to seek God on our own. We are pulling down the decaying walls of our inherited religious structures one by one and putting in place a personal spirituality that at last would establish and keep us in connection with our Source. Thus joined, the closer we get in the embrace of the living, breathing, loving Creator Energy, the nearer we come to answering the eternal questions. Your personal spiritual path, however you decide to build it and walk it, is taking you to the heart of the sacred mystery: to know what your life means in the world. Each of us finds our unique knowing, and yet for all of us it is the same.

The bold new iconography of earth's place among the stars may be giving us a clue to our individual and collective purpose. First and most obvious among the new set of insights dawning in us is the utter illusion of separation. Wherever we draw political lines on a map, wherever we build walls to keep ourselves protected within and keep others out, boundaries are nonexistent from the perspective of a few hundred miles out. Looking from the outside, we see there are no separate nations, creeds, philosophies, ethnicities, or any other real or imagined partitions. We are a whole, as we can now plainly see, and this true picture of unity is leading us back to the metaphysical meanderings of the mystics, where connection between you and me and between our Source and us has always been the basis of their rapturous revelations. In a way, the mystics anticipated in their spiritual visions the truth of planetary unity we are now seeing in photographs from space.

Among the modern mystics leading us to understand the principle of oneness is the late Joel Goldsmith, whose thought evolved out of Christian Science, where he was a successful practitioner for a number of years. Born into a Jewish family in

1892, Joel left school and traveled around the world, eventually becoming a businessman. After his experiences as a Marine in World War I, he looked for a spiritual path that would somehow address the problem of man's inhumanity to man. For him, Christian Science was that path. Gradually, through meditation and studies of the sacred scriptures of the world, he developed his own mystical philosophy, which he called the Infinite Way. In 1948, as he was settling into a well-earned retirement, his book *The Infinite Way* was published, launching him on a new career in teaching and spiritual healing that lasted until his death in 1964. His lectures were recorded on audiotape and edited into several books, which sold millions of copies.

I discovered Joel (his students almost never referred to him by his last name, only "Joel") through one of my spiritual teachers, Hazel Archer, about whom I spoke earlier. I was going through a particularly trying time after the death of my mother, when Hazel sat me down and had me listen to a tape of one of Joel's lectures. In it, he speaks about the parable of the prodigal son from the New Testament. I did not want to hear anything from the Bible at that time; I was soured on all so-called divine revelations in books. God had done nothing to save my mother or console me at her loss. But as I listened to Joel's telling of the story and heard his profound interpretation, something came alive in me. I recognized what he was saying as pure spiritual truth and knew I wanted to become a student of his work.

He begins by laying out the familiar account of the wealthy landowner who had two sons, the elder of which stays with him, while the younger goes off and fritters away his inheritance. After a time, the young man returns home to the father's wildly enthusiastic reception. The elder brother, out in the fields super-vising workers, hears that his father has ordered a feast. He is furious and hurt, and refuses to go in to greet his brother.

So his father goes out and pleads with him. But he answers his father, "Look! All these years I've been slaving for you and never disobeyed your orders. Yet you never gave me even a young goat so I could celebrate with my friends. But when this son of yours who has squandered your property with prostitutes comes home, you kill the fattened calf for him!" "My son," the father says, "you are always with me, and everything I have is yours. But we must celebrate and be glad, because this brother of yours was dead and is alive again; he was lost and is found" (Luke 15:11–32).

On the tape, Joel completely ignores the traditional point and lesson of the story—that God (the landowner) is always ready and willing to forgive human wrongdoings (the prodigal)—and focuses instead on the father's words to the elder brother: "Son, you are always with me, and everything I have is yours." On this one line, he hangs his entire mystical vision of unity with the Source. We are already and always have been with the Source, and so everything the Source has we also have. It is a majestic insight that goes to the very soul of mystical connection in the unity of consciousness.

In Joel Goldsmith's dazzling vision, "there is nothing but God," and therefore we are all one in the oneness of the Source. We get to that awareness directly and personally through a med-itation practice, which is an emptying, a listening, and a waiting for words, ideas, or feelings of instruction and assurance from the Source Itself. These contacts from the Source can come at any time, whether in the temple of a listening meditation or in the marketplace of a busy workday. This is from his book *The Thunder of Silence*: "All that the Father has is now flowing through us out into this world as a divine Grace. . . . If we attain the consciousness of God, we discover that there is nothing but God—God appearing as flowers, God appearing as food on our table, God appearing as the clothing on our backs, God appearing as harmonious relationships, God appearing as the perfect functioning of our minds and bodies. . . . There is no higher goal attainable on earth than an inner communication with this Presence that never leaves us nor forsakes us."

"Divine love always has met and always will meet every human need," Mary Baker Eddy, the founder of Christian Science, writes in *Science and Health with Key to the Scriptures* (1875). Joel goes the next step to the actual experience of contact with what he called "the source of all supply." His teachings are an invitation for each of us to be a mystic, or rather to get more in touch with our natural mystic abilities. After we have left the confines of religion, questioned everything, taken with us what we could practically use, cleaned up our emotional and mental acts, and forged our own spiritual path, what is left is direct connection to the Source. It is available to ordinary people like you and me, if we will take the time and make the effort by emptying ourselves and allowing the tidal wave of grace already welling up in us to flow forth. The awareness of the presence of the Source in and with us also brings about what appear to be spontaneous healings everywhere around us, but they are in fact the correct natural state of things.

For twenty-five years now, I have been studying Joel's work in small meditation groups and on my own, and I am still mining the jewels in his vision. It contains so many of the elements I yearned for in my spiritual search within the monastery and after I left it. The purity of this direct spiritual approach, without rules, dogmas, or intermediaries, reminded me of the cosmic theology of Teilhard. If what you have just read about Joel Goldsmith sparks something in your heart, you may want to look into the Infinite Way work. Remember that he comes out of a Christian tradition; you may have to sort through all the specifically Bible-bound terminology to get to the spiritual nuggets. However, Joel uses Christian scriptures not as a Billy Graham–type preacher but more as a Joseph Campbell–type tutor and mentor, pointing out the eternal truths behind the myths.

I have always been struck by the way mystics die. Joel was teaching classes in London in 1964. They were a series of closed classes to longtime students and followers of his spiritual philosophy. After one of these classes, a small group went with Joel back to his hotel suite to have some refreshments and continue their discussions. About an hour later, Joel said he wanted to go into the bedroom to lie down a bit, but that he would be back shortly. He stretched out on the bed, closed his eyes, and died.

A few years ago I heard a tape of the final talk by Thomas Merton, the Trappist contemplative who was probably the most famous monk in the world in the 1950s and 1960s. Most obituaries carry the ambiguous line that he died "as a result of an accident in Thailand." This is what happened.

Merton rarely left his monastery, the austere, aptly named Gethsemani in Kentucky; monks there take the vow of stability, promising to live in their monastery all their lives. But in 1968 he was invited to address an important ecumenical meeting of Catholic and Buddhist monks in Bangkok. Granted permission from his abbot, Merton left Gethsemani and traveled half way around the world to the conference.

The day was December 10, the twenty-seventh anniversary of Merton's entrance into the Abbey of Gethsemani. On the tape, his talk to the other monks is quite moving, full of soulful reflections on the practice of monasticism and the monk's role in the modern world. The meeting schedule called for a rest break between his morning presentation and an afternoon session, also featuring Merton. He returned to his room and took a shower; stepping out onto the wet stone floor, he stumbled against a defectively wired fan and electrocuted himself. At the end of the morning session, which turned out to be the end of his life, as well, the tape caught his last jocular words: "I've said enough for now—I'm going to disappear for a while."

Disappear, not die. Going to lie down a bit and will be back, not die. When we are aware of the presence of the Source in us, Joel Goldsmith says, "In that very moment, the illusory appearances of sin, disease, death, lack, and limitation evaporate." Death, in particular, assumes the quality of illusion in all mystic writings. It is as if the mystic is already living as Teilhard de Chardin proposed for us all, as "spiritual beings on a human journey." From this vantage point the twin temporal brackets of birth and death in the flesh are merely passage points marking different ways for the soul to express itself.

{ .. .. }

The new iconography of our earthly home reveals the mystic vision of the oneness of all. I believe the NASA photographs, which continue to come in practically every day from our space probes and from the Hubble Space Telescope, are changing us fundamentally. They are pushing us toward the unity of existence glimpsed until now only by the spiritual seers, making mystics of you and me, and everyone else on earth.

As these awe-inspiring images of ourselves from outside ourselves—images of wholeness—sink into our consciousness and settle into our imagination, we are likely to see our sense of separation from one another and from our Source, as old as Adam and Eve, gradually "evaporate," to use Joel's word. The answer to the question of how to bring about world peace, end hunger, heal disease, stop inequality, and resolve the rest of the world's problems may be to allow these inspiring new depictions of our planetary home to do their magical work in the human imagination. Seeing our terrestrial island's closed system and understanding what it suggests, we may find a worldwide sense of personal responsibility emerging on its own, quite naturally.

"If humankind would accept and acknowledge this responsibility and become creatively engaged in the process of evolution, consciously as well as unconsciously," Jonas Salk tells us, "a new reality would emerge, and a new age could be born." Your personal spiritual path is leading you ever closer to the meaning of your life, and of all life. It appears to be converging at the place where you recognize with the mystics that every one of us is part of a vast cosmic whole. The end and purpose of our spiritual search may be this realization that we are all one, so we can act on that awareness by living in alignment with it. "The sense of soul comes out of your relationship with the world," writes Yorkshire poet David Whyte. "It is not just you, by yourself. It's your relationship to the world." What remains, then, for the spiritual seeker on the path to live always and everywhere connected to the Source of life?

While researching the subject of miracles a few years ago, I came across the story of a German doctor who visited Lourdes in southwestern France toward the end of the nineteenth century. He did not come for a cure but to make a scientific inquiry into the claims of spontaneous healings at the famous grotto where Mary, the mother of Jesus, was said to have appeared in 1858. By that time, thousands had told of miracles happening to them. In its usual cautious way, the Catholic Church authenticated only a few (so far, after 150 years and scores of millions of pilgrims, it has confirmed only sixty-seven). The doctor took the handful of undisputed cases, studied the medical records, and conducted interviews with the subjects, their physicians and nurses, and eyewitnesses. Satisfied with the facts of the healings, he then set out to find one thread that might hold them all together. After another year of investigation, he reported the only common element in the miracles: at the moment of cure, the person receiving the spontaneous healing was praying for the healing of someone else.

In the mystical vision of the unity of all, as you perform some action it influences the rest of us down to our very being. This is why the only reasonable kind of action for the person following a spiritual path to take must end in service. You want only what is good for you, so you do good to others, knowing that from the vision of unity you are doing it for yourself. When the spiritual teachers through the centuries tell us that to serve is to live the fullness of the spiritual life, they are coming from that deeply grasped place of oneness.

{ .. .. }

Service. Reading the word, you may wonder how this thing
called service would unfold in your life, busy as it is, devoted as
it is to your own pressing pursuits. Am I talking about leaving
your job to tend to the poor in Calcutta? Am I suggesting you
stop looking after your family and start teaching villagers in
Peru how to build a solid waste management system? Strange
how our thoughts immediately jump to the literal and the
obvious when service is mentioned. I think it frightens us in a
way. Automatically, we assume that to be of service we have to
leave the life we are living and take up something else entirely—
and the something else, in our minds, is usually lower, poorer,
and harder. Surely the spiritual meaning of service does not
require a career or lifestyle change. It may require only a shift
in how you view your life and its place in the world.

Albert Schweitzer, the French physician and philosopher who
spent most of his life as a medical missionary in Gabon in sub-
Saharan Africa, spoke to a group of young people in the 1950s,
saying, "I don't know what your destiny will be, but one thing I
do know—the only ones among you who will be really happy are
those who have sought and found how to serve." Service is the
crown of the spiritual life. The path you create for yourself must
lead here, because service is the key that unlocks the secret door
behind which is the answer to your life's meaning and purpose. It
is through service to others that you find why you are here on this
particular planet in this particular body at this particular time.

A spiritual path that does not connect to the idea of service
is not a spiritual path at all. It is just plain old narcissism dressed
up in cardboard angel wings and a fake halo. You have seen these

people at personal growth workshops and classes, hungry for
the next spiritual morsel. They seem to think that making themselves "spiritual," whatever that means, is an end in itself. Scratch
the veneer of spiritual narcissists and you will find self-involved
little Calvinists trying hard to improve themselves and forget
everyone else. They are missing the whole point of this earthly
sojourn. If the path is to make any sense at all, it has to lead
out and away from you, where it can intersect with the paths
of others—which, of course, is the same grand path.

An Albert Schweitzer fulfills both the letter and the spirit of
service. Mother Teresa, Mohandas Gandhi, Martin Luther King,
Nelson Mandela, and the other well-known humanitarians do
the same. There is another approach to service. It is more like an
attitude: you continue doing what you are doing and lift it to the
spiritual level by making the intention to do all that you do in
the service of others. This is a service mind-set, a way of framing
all your actions with the awareness that you are part of everyone
and everyone is part of you. If this sounds suspiciously like the
Golden Rule, or the advice of Sankara, Buddha, Jesus, and the
other spiritual lights down the ages, it is exactly that. Remember:
they had the vision of wholeness, and from it their lives emptied
out in service.

"I never perfected an invention that I did not think about in
terms of the service it might give others," Thomas Edison told his
biographer late in life. "I find out what the world needs, then I
proceed to invent." Think of what our lives would be like without
the electric light bulb. Edison's spiritual path of service did not
lead him out of his laboratory to feed the poor of the world. He
stayed there at the workbench, in time amassing patents for more
than a thousand inventions to improve the quality of people's

Service

lives. His attitude of service raised all he invented to what Hazel Archer called "high humanitarianism."

When I was head of the film school in Santa Fe, students (especially graduating seniors) would come to me with the Big Question—"What do I do now?"—and its attendant cry: "Help!" The problem of what kind of career to follow almost always had a financial frame around it. They could buy some secondhand film equipment or a video camera and go out and make meaningful documentaries on subjects they were passionate about, or they could go to Hollywood and get a job in the movies, work hard and become like Steven Spielberg and make trillions of dollars. One student who considered herself highly evolved thought the Spielberg option was the better one, because then she could "give a lot of money to the poor."

Invariably, I had to remind them that making life decisions solely on the basis of getting and spending money could lead them to make bad choices, and they would wake up at forty unhappy and shopping for a psychiatrist instead of a new BMW. I asked them to think about rephrasing their question from "How much can I get for my work?" to "What can I contribute to the world?" Most of them, true to their consumer conditioning (which regards self-worth as a banking issue), shrugged their shoulders and left my office intent on accumulating the maximum amount of money in the minimum length of time.

"Success is not the key to happiness—happiness is the key to success," Schweitzer reminds us. "If you love what you are doing, you will be successful." You have heard that, or variants of it, many times before. Joseph Campbell says it as "Follow your bliss! When you follow your bliss, doors will open where you would not have thought there would be doors; and where there

wouldn't be a door for anyone else." You discover your life's
meaning and purpose through your work in the world, your
service; you know you are doing right service by the amount
of profound, true happiness it brings you. Wherever your spiritual path is taking you, it must end in fulfillment of your highest
potential through service to others.

There is a deeper meaning of service, and it loops back to
the principle of oneness. I was surprised to hear on one of Joel
Goldsmith's tapes that he did not support one cause over
another, whether it was political or religious or philosophical.
Nor did he write to his senator, circulate petitions, march in
defense of or against anything, advocate positions, fire off letters to the editor, or stuff envelopes for a candidate. He did not
lift his hand to change anything in the day-to-day world but
preferred instead to spend his time teaching and contemplating
the oneness of all things. I thought about the Buddha, who sat
under the Bodhi tree in meditation while all around him followers swirled, busily gathering and giving alms; for the Buddha, contemplating the principle of unity was enough. I
thought also about Jesus, who, when he was rebuked by one
of his students for allowing a woman to lavish expensive oil on
his feet instead of selling it and giving the money to the poor,
snapped, "The poor you have always with you"—ending the
discussion.

Certainly I am not suggesting that you and I should not stop
to help another human being when the need presents itself, or
not work to alleviate suffering or improve social conditions and
the environment. These should be self-evident opportunities for
service to the seeker on a spiritual path. However, if our rescuing
or crusading or healing activities are not inspired by our mystic

Service

understanding of the oneness of all, they may degenerate into empty expressions of self-involvement.

Albert Einstein saw each of us as a part of the whole, which we call universe, a part limited in time and space, experiencing ourselves "as something separate from the rest." It is a kind of optical delusion of personal consciousness. "This delusion is a . . . prison for us. Our task must be to free ourselves from this prison by widening our circle of compassion to embrace all living creatures and the whole of nature in its beauty."

Consciousness is one, and so your individual consciousness comprises all of consciousness. Joel says on one tape, "When I sit and practice the Presence, aware of my indissoluble connection with God, I raise all creation to that awareness." Our spiritual path leads to the radiant conclusion that the bond between our Source and us has never been broken; what we have been seeking has been here all the while ("you are always with me, and everything I have is yours").

The spellbinding picture of the earth from the surface of our nearest cosmic neighbor, the first earthrise in our two-million-year history on this planet, may signal that we are ready to assume new responsibilities that go beyond our individual selves. It may be urging us to participate in an emerging global mind and global heart. A global soul, as well, for when we are connected to the Source of all life wherever we stand is holy ground, a sacred site, and we raise the living soil under our feet to a sacramental substance. Meanwhile, we strive to walk a spiritual path of our own making, to live simply, to live detached, to live responsibly, as mystics in a world that is flying on the wings of ever-unfolding consciousness, inexorably back to a home we have never left.

CHAPTER TWELVE

heaven on earth

And oh if there be an Elysium on earth,
It is this, it is this!
—THOMAS MOORE (1779–1852), "THE LIGHT OF THE HAREM"

YOU AND I are sitting on a bench in a shady park at our university, watching our tethered horses lap up water from a wooden trough. We are in a small town in the south of Spain. The year is 1491. Our talk is about current events. Word has arrived that Captain Diego Cao of neighboring Portugal has sailed south along the African coast and landed at the mouth of the Zaire River, gateway to the gigantic kingdom of Kongo. Among other evidence of his visit to that strange land, he has brought back something called bananas.

You ask my opinion about these reckless voyages of exploration we have been hearing about. I say the adventurers are

flirting with dangers beyond the human imagination. As everyone in Europe well knows, the world we live on is a tabletop,
and if a ship sails out too far from land, it will disappear over
the edge of water's end and monsters will devour its passengers.
You agree, of course. In our worldview, the ground we are standing on is—as would be perfectly obvious to even a fool—flat and
stationary, and the sun, moon, and stars rise and set over it.

Flash forward. Now it is the year 1591. You and I are sitting
together on that same bench in the shade in our little town.
Again, we are discussing the subject of exploration. Amazing
reports have been reaching us about wonderful, exotic places
we had not heard of before. Since the voyages of Christopher
Columbus a century ago, the whole world has opened up, it
seems. Dozens of explorers from our own country have sailed
out to sea farther than any European before them and returned
home; they did not fall into an abyss. Something else: they sailed
west and reached the east. Obviously, we live on the surface of a
sphere, not a tabletop.

The flat world of our grandparents has been stood on end,
replaced by a round one. When a while back, in 1543, Nicolas
Copernicus published his treatise *Revolutionibus Orbium
Coelestium,* with its proposition that the earth orbits the sun,
it was a jolt. Then just a few years ago, Giordano Bruno's *On
the Infinite Universe and Its Worlds* suggested that the universe
is infinitely large and that the earth is by no means at the center
of it. He was burned at the stake for the idea, but it seems to
have taken hold anyway. As our contemporary, the English
playwright William Shakespeare, would say, this is a brave new
world indeed.

⟨ .. .. ⟩

Earlier, I mentioned paradigm shift theory as applied to human evolution, the idea that after a lengthy period of plateau how we think about ourselves and our world changes abruptly and dramatically. The Middle Ages in Europe, for instance, was a time of paradigm stability. In a heartbeat of history, everything changed. The very ground people stood on was not the same—actually, it was the opposite of what everyone had thought. What caused this tremendous shift, so pervasive that the generations born after it saw the world in a radically different way from their parents and grandparents?

The easy answer is that a few explorers decided to test the prevailing flat-earth belief. Paradigm shift advocates would suggest that the leap in consciousness from flat world to round world might have come before anyone set out on a voyage of exploration. In this scenario, exciting changes were in the air and explorers became passionately consumed with the idea of sailing out past the limits of the known world. Their voyages were not a cause but a confirmation of the dawning paradigm shift.

Whether the stunning shift in consciousness in the sixteenth century preceded or was the result of new discoveries describing reality in a new way, nothing was the same after it happened. Once it was over, humankind made a huge lunge forward.

Today we appear to be living on the cusp of another paradigm shift, one that promises to be every bit as earth-shattering as the shift that took people from the Middle Ages to the Renaissance and the Enlightenment. Depending on whom you listen to—theoretical physicists, cultural anthropologists, climatologists, astrologers, shamans, even hyperventilating evangelicals of the left-behind persuasion—an enormous movement in consciousness is upon us. Whether we are directing the shift or following it into an uncharted future, all indications are that we are just about to undergo, or have begun and are earnestly engaged in, a major transformation of our collective worldview.

Change is in the air, as it was at the beginning of the sixteenth century. Scientists are telling us that our long-held beliefs about the space-time-energy construction of our universe may be incomplete and overly simple. To find out who or what we are, we have been observing, measuring, and weighing the physical universe. In 2000, it was announced that at last we have a working draft of the human genome, the set of genetic instructions that governs the assembly and function of all human beings. It was a dazzling discovery, the end of the long search for our definitive material makeup. However, there is more to us than mere chemical processes. For many scientists, the world "in here" has become as important as or more important than the world "out there." They are poised to begin seeking answers to the elemental questions of life in places it cannot see, calculate, or quantify—the world of consciousness, of memory, of intuition, of dreams.

One interesting development in the new physics is a series of scientific experiments in the early 1980s characterized by the term "entanglement." When two or more particles of matter interact with one another, a bond is formed. From then on, a correlation will always exist between them. Even if particles are at opposite ends of the universe, they will be in a state of "non-separability." If all matter emerged from energy in the singularity of the big bang, then the implication is that all is one. This sounds suspiciously like a spiritual principle, the ages-old vision of the mystics.

Wherever this immanent paradigm shift lands us, it is likely to alter radically how we relate to our Source. To get closer to answering the question of where we came from, for instance, it is clear that we may need to revisit our Western creation myth, which is about separation, control, and dominance, and then think about replacing it with a more appropriate story that speaks of unity, compassion, responsibility, and love.

I always thought this inevitable business of having to demolish our Adam and Eve creation myth lay somewhere in the dim future, but unconscious (to be charitable) forces have conspired to do it in our own day. During the two recent Iraq wars, we turned into a moonscape of bombed-out craters the area between the Tigris and Euphrates Rivers, the so-called Cradle of Civilization, and near it the legendary location of the Garden of Eden. We also burned the Iraq National Library and Archives to the ground in 2003; they held the carved and written records of our culture's inception. Additionally, we allowed (witnesses said we encouraged) the looting of the National Museum in Baghdad, destroying 80 percent of its holdings going back to the dawn of Western culture. The symbolism, though crude, is inescapable.

The monotheistic religions of Judaism, Christianity, and Islam all began with a man named Abraham in about 2000 B.C. Abraham lived in Ur of the Chaldees, a Sumerian city in what is present-day Iraq, about 235 miles southeast of Baghdad. Ur was famous for its huge ziggurat, or stepped tower, completed a century before Abraham was born. The ancient structure is still standing, one of its walls now defaced in spray paint with a big "Semper Fi," the slogan of the U.S. Marines; a few miles away is the newly constructed Tallil Airbase, where a Burger King and Pizza Hut serve the needs of armed forces personnel. It was here that the One God appeared to Abraham and told him to found a clan that would become a nation, and that would be dedicated to him alone above all other gods.

Over the next eight hundred years, the Hebrews, as Abraham's descendants were called, wandered the Middle East looking for a land promised them as part of their pact with the One God. Around 1200 B.C., one of their leaders, Moses, brought them to it—Canaan, which is more or less modern Israel and some of its surrounding area. Tradition tells us that Moses is also the author of the five opening books of what became the Bible, the first of which is the "seed-plot" book, Genesis, containing the origin story of the Hebrews and the rest of humankind.

Much has been written about the Book of Genesis, and especially the first two chapters, which contain quite different accounts of creation but with similar implications. Briefly, God, who turns out to be the One God of Abraham, creates the world and then fashions a man, and as a kind of afterthought a woman, to live in it and "be fruitful, and multiply, and replenish the earth, and subdue it; and have dominion over the fish of the sea, and over the fowl of the air, and over the cattle, and over all the earth, and over every creeping thing that creepeth upon the earth. . . ."

The divine command to subdue, have dominion over, and populate the earth has gotten us into a great deal of trouble through the centuries, and just now we are about at the breaking point in what the earth can handle. Over four millennia of adhering to God's go-ahead-have-it-all counsel, we have made a toxic waste dump of our planetary garden. We have forgotten the replenish-the-earth part, systematically plundering and destroying our natural resources and befouling our rivers, lakes, oceans, and the very air we inhale to sustain life. Now we are seeing the results of this species arrogance in alarming climate change, elevated disease rates, endless famine, unstoppable pandemics, unprecedented natural disasters from global warming, and all the other ills that beset us and are related directly to our irresponsible human behavior.

That is not all. Lurking in the shadows of Genesis is a chilling sense of separation, beginning with the separation of the genders. It then extends also to the woman and the serpent, the tree of the knowledge of good and evil, the farmer Cain and the shepherd Abel, being naked (sinless) and being clothed (sinful), Noah and his family as separate from everybody else, and so on. "And I will put enmity between you and the woman, and between your offspring and hers; he will crush your head, and you will strike his heel" (Genesis 3:15). "I will make you into a great nation and I will bless you. . . . I will bless those who bless you, and whoever curses you I will curse" (Genesis 12:2–3). Separation from the beginning: "In the beginning God created the heaven and the earth" (Genesis 1:1). If you were looking for a first cause of our long-standing sense of separation from the divine Source, the Bible would be it.

For centuries, the minds of most of us did not appear to have the capacity to see through the self-destructive philosophy of our precious cultural heritage. But today many of us are waking up to the tragic shortcomings of this long-held worldview and are seeing the necessity of creating a new way of perceiving our Source, our common destiny, and ourselves. Part of the paradigm shift we are living through involves coming up with a new story about our origins and our future. The new myth will not be something we invent, I am thinking, but something we remember from our primeval past. Various events will erupt like little mushrooms—nations falling, economies collapsing, cultures absorbing each other, tectonic plates yawning and stretching, antichrists appearing, flying saucers landing, whatever—and when the dust settles we will see the "new" narrative of ourselves as if it had been there for eons, which it has. All this will happen naturally, just as in 1591 a new round-world matrix emerged without you and me, on our park bench, doing anything to bring it about.

We may have an indication of what lies beyond the new paradigm shift from the area of inquiry science, on tiptoes, is just beginning to explore. Astrology, long discredited by the modern world, is starting to reclaim the position it held in antiquity as a tool for plumbing the depths of the human experience. Relevant to the discussion of paradigm shift, astrology tells us that we are living through the end of one cosmic epoch and the beginning of another.

We have been hearing about the age of Aquarius at least since 1968, when the Broadway musical *Hair* popularized it as a coming time when "love will steer the stars." The great ages are technical astrological terms for periods of time, based on what are called the precessions of equinoxes. Earth's slight wobble causes the fixed stars to rise and set against our solar years in a minute rotation, so that on the first day of spring the constellation of Aries no longer rises, as it did in the time of the Roman Republic. Instead the constellation of Pisces now rises on that day (precession goes backward through the zodiac). Astrologers put the measurement of each age on this star clock as 2,160 years long—25,920 for a complete cycle through the twelve houses of the zodiac.

As precise as this looks, there still is plenty of room for interpretive maneuvers. We know we are leaving the age of Pisces and going into the age of Aquarius, but exactly when the new age will dawn is a matter of opinion. The age of Pisces, the sign of the two fish, was a time when people were ruled more by their emotions than their intellect. It was also a period influenced in an essential way by dualities and the struggle of opposites; the two fish of the Pisces symbol swim in opposite directions. Conflict between opposing ideologies was the dominant model: dogmatic Christianity struggled against equally dogmatic atheistic materialism, democracies locked horns with monarchies, and science battled religion.

Some astrologers suggest that the first thousand years of an age embody the more positive aspects of the prevailing sign's influence, and the second half the more negative aspects. Looking back at the two millennia just past, we might conclude the same. Christianity, pristine and unchurched at the start of the age of Pisces (the fish was the earliest symbol for the Christ), ushered in a period of unconditional love, a constructive Piscean quality; the second millennia was devoted to irreconcilable conflict, a destructive one.

Any of a number of recent world events would qualify as a definitive sign that the age of Pisces is ending. The collapse in 1991 of the Soviet Union, founded upon an ideology of social conflict, is one. Another might be the erosion of the big religions; in Europe at least, the pews are empty. In our own country, Watergate (Pisces is a water sign), which unmasked a government of secrecy, corruption, and conflict, is still another. I suppose it goes without saying that the symbolism around September 11, 2001, also speaks to the end of the Piscean period. The twin towers were like two opposing fish hovering above the water at the lower tip of Manhattan. The World Trade Center may be the center of the place—ground zero—where we traded one worldview for another. I will leave it to the disciples of Erich Von Daniken to finish the analogy.

Certainly, the invention of voice and image electronic broadcasting (Aquarius is an air sign), computers, and their spin-off gadgets and the development of the Internet are unquestionably Aquarian hallmarks, as are the unification of Europe, the rise of alternative medicine, global humanitarian responses to natural disasters, and tireless exploration of space by robotic telescopes and cameras, suggesting that the new age is here already. Granted we are still killing each other in conflicts over bankrupt ideologies and dusty religious beliefs all over the planet. But we may be living through a period of overlap between an age of strife fueled by emotions run rampant and (we trust) a saner, more rational, more benevolent time.

The age of Aquarius exists in our imagination as an era of reason, unity, and altruism. However, those are only some of the expressions of Aquarian energy. I asked Diane Eichenbaum,

the well-known metaphysical astrologer (*Soul Signs*), about this
and she reminded me that the age of Aquarius is predisposed to
bring with it as well cold intellectualism and denial of feelings,
defiant individuality and rebelliousness, unpredictability, eccen-
tricity, and perversity. "It will not necessarily be a bed of roses,"
she says, even though fresh new ideas will fly around, unbound
by doctrines and dogmas. The spirit of the age will be freedom,
selflessness, innovation, cooperation—as the song says, "harmony and understanding / sympathy and trust abounding,"
but only with some effort on our part.

I say "on our part" because you and I are now positioned
to help drive our collective evolution into higher realms of consciousness. Teilhard de Chardin envisioned this dramatic moment
in human history as the opportunity for humanity to assume
full responsibility for lifting our home planet, and all of us on it,
up one more rung on the evolutionary ladder. This step will lead
eventually to the omega point of universal history, ultimate
ecstatic union with our Source. If this sounds like a task too
lofty and too mighty, impractical for us as a species, impossible
for us as individuals, we can rest assured: all that is required of
us to move the cosmic mountain is to love one another and, as
the hippies used to say, go with the flow.

{ .. .. }

One golden afternoon in early fall, I sat with Hazel Parcells on
the porch of her ranch house in Sapello, New Mexico. She had
just turned 106, and maybe she had a sense already that this
would be her last autumn. She spoke about the great cycles of
planetary time and the human seed that had found its way on

a turn of the wheel of the ages to the fertile soil of earth. "I have never thought of the Garden of Eden as a place we fell from," she said, "but as a place we are aspiring to." The way she saw it, our human species was moving ever upward in self-awareness to the point where we would be able to rediscover and acknowledge our planetary home and embrace it as a child embraces its loving mother. In this embrace, we would create together a beautiful and bountiful garden, with us contributing our evolving spiritual consciousness and mother earth contributing the sacred material substance of our being.

The planet as a garden is a comforting image, one that connects well to our Aquarian longings and capabilities. In the coming age, we could find ourselves more firmly planted here, using our glittering technology to turn earth to a literal garden as well as a preserve for fantastic ideas and brilliant imaginings; Aquarius is the sign of the genius. As our manned space programs began to crumble away in a series of disastrous failures, I believed it was a signal that we may be prepared to stay here on the home planet after all. For many years—centuries, it seems—the popular imagination has been pointing us toward abandoning our planetary crib after soiling it beyond reclamation. In *Mexico Mystique: The Coming Sixth World of Consciousness* (1975), Frank Waters asks the question, "Are we on this ecologically doomed planet psychologically making efforts to leave it? Is this the unconscious prompting, akin to the instinct of migrating birds—or rats deserting a sinking ship!—behind our rationally engineered landings on the moon and preparations to extend our space travel to Mars?"

A few years ago, the answer to that rhetorical question, which Waters delivered with the authority of a prophet, would have been an obvious and resounding yes. But something is shifting.

I find it hopeful that we appear to be giving up on sending human bodies to the stars. These meat machines, as inventor Nikola Tesla called them, are entirely unsuitable for traveling to and living on other planets. In the years to come, I believe we will be training ourselves to make expeditions to distant galaxies in our minds. We already go there in our dreams. Scientists are researching diligently in the field of lucid or controlled dreaming. It is just a matter of time before we perfect skills like out-of-body travel, astral projection, and remote viewing (now exploited by the CIA to find hidden warheads in China) and use them to explore "out there" while processing it all "in here."

Religion has always drawn our attention away from the earth toward an imaginary heaven (ironically, full of earthly delights). Christian tradition is based on the belief that we are made for heaven, not earth. We are just passing through this impermanent shadowy world on the way to eternal bliss or eternal torment. Life on earth is a vale of tears, as we trudge through the difficult, sometimes insurmountable tests, suffering this planet's slings and arrows because at the end it will get us into heaven. Call it a theology of escape, pure and simple, encouraging us not to stay here and tend our splendid garden home but to renounce, suppress, and disdain it on our way to a better place. The sky-God religions, in particular, have kept our eyes fixed on the heavens; earth was synonymous with our lower nature, sin, and death.

Fortunately, religion looks to be going the way of all the other bloated, useless institutions of the previous age—and with it the concept of earth as a waiting room for heaven—which, since we do not actually live here, we can go ahead and trash. You would not think religion is leaving the world stage, hearing about megachurches in the Bible Belt and televangelists with

Heaven on Earth

followings in the millions (and bank accounts to match). But all this sounds like the last loud gasps of a dying dinosaur. "Every form of culture, in its vanishing, receives its most elaborate and intense expression," says cultural historian William Irwin Thompson in his prescient *The Time Falling Bodies Take to Light* (1981). What could be more elaborate and intense than lunatic calls to "Blow them [Muslim terrorists] all away in the name of the Lord!" (the Rev. Jerry Falwell on CNN)? Or, for that matter, flying airplanes into skyscrapers in the name of Allah? For organized religion, this could indeed be the end time it has been predicting obsessively. Its *own* apocalypse is now.

The spirituality of the future will spring from our reverence for the planet. Before God was a father in the sky, she was a mother in the earth. Riane Eisler, in her pioneering cultural history *The Chalice and the Blade* (1987), tells us that the first religions, if you can call them that, were simply a way of life with bodies of ritual connected to the earth, its movements through time and space, its amazing seasons, its miraculous fecundity. They were mother religions, honoring the earth itself as the divine source of life. In this goddess-inspired world, Eisler says, the social pattern was one of partnership—between humans and nature, between women and men, between neighbors—rather than the one we have now and have had at least since the time of the God of Abraham: the dominator pattern. Under the dominator model, there is a pyramidal hierarchy where the people at the top have more than the people have who are below them, and they exert power over them.

If Eisler's partnership realm sounds like life in the Garden of Eden before the "fall," it may be exactly that. The Neolithic or agrarian age (the Garden) lasted from approximately 8000 B.C. to roughly 2000 B.C., when barbarians from the north and east descended gradually on the highly developed goddess civilizations in the Middle East. When they did, they brought with them the domination of men over women, and thus in their religious expression the domination of the sky father god over the earth mother goddess. People stopped building mounds of earth to symbolize the fertile, pregnant earth mother and began constructing pyramids flanked by phallic obelisks and towered temples with steps their priests would climb to the sky. Could our Western culture, constantly churning with belligerent turmoil, be nothing more at root than a barbaric aberration, a detour from the straight path of human evolution? If so, the turning of the age at hand may be bringing us back in line with our original course of development after four millennia of domination delusions.

I like the idea that the propensity toward evil may not be a true trait of human nature but something that came in quite uninvited with our barbarian ancestors. Maybe we really are the "little less than the angels" of our spiritual folklore, bent more on doing good to each other and ourselves than bad. If so, we may be ready to resume the work of the world we began so long ago, building the conscious, thinking, self-reflecting layer of our garden planet. We were busily engaged in creating heaven on earth when fear and mutual mistrust cruelly interrupted us. Now we have an opportunity to rewrite the ending of our creation myth and reimagine our human destiny. In this version, we are not cast outside the gates of paradise by an avenging angel but are at home among the lush forests, waterfalls, mountains, and meadows of our earthly garden, and we walk with God in the cool of the evening.

Joel Goldsmith says, "The lion will lie down with the lamb—when we have ended our malpractice of the lion." We who have been looking for God find that the divine Source is right where we have been standing. We did not see it because we were off imagining ourselves as separate from it, and separate from one another. But that sense of separation is a mirage, and to adhere to it is spiritual "malpractice." Our personal spiritual path takes us not to some far-off heaven beyond the stars but back to the heaven of this planet, our divine mother, from whence we came. Like her, we are three-quarters water. Our bodies are made up of the same minerals and other chemical elements as her body. We are the earth. Firmly and joyfully here, we can probe the endless mystery of life: how it begins, how it changes, how it is reborn as we embrace ever closer the Great Mother that has been with us down the ages as Gaia, Ishtar, Isis, Izanami, Demeter, Hu-Tu, Itzpapalotl, Spider-Woman, Magna Mater, the Virgin Mary.

When you seek God on your own, you end here in the magic garden contemplating with awe the miracle of life, honoring it in all its cycles, its amazing ways, its magnificent moods and swells and shifts. The answers to the eternal questions of Who am I? Where did I come from? Where am I going? are here in this sacred place. You and I hold the future—not merely our personal future, but our collective human future—in the palm of our hand. By living in integrity, with impeccability, connected with each other as children of a loving mother, we can direct the next stage in our evolutionary process upward, spiritualizing the planet as we go.

AFTERWORD

The day will come when, after harnessing space, the winds, the
tides, gravitation, we shall harness for God the energies of love.
  And, on that day, for the second time in the history of the
world, man will have discovered fire.
—PIERRE TEILHARD DE CHARDIN, *THE EVOLUTION OF CHASTITY*

LOOKING BACK over these pages, I see that the primary focus
has been creating a spiritual path for yourself outside religion
and doing it completely on your own. As you know by now,
I believe strongly that you and I are being called at this important moment in history to take full responsibility for our spiritual lives. This means not relying anymore on the codified
answers to the eternal questions thrust upon us by religious
structures of the past. We are being helped along in this process
by the spirit of the times, in which we are witnessing a changing of the cosmic guard from an old paradigm to a new one in
all areas of human life. In relating to our Source, collectively
and personally we appear to have reached the end of the age
of religion and are about to begin the age of spirituality. Every
indication is that organized religion, with its inherent divisive-
ness, will have to pass from the human scene if we are ever to
grow into an authentic spiritual adulthood.

But creating a meaningful and rewarding personal spirituality need not be a solitary venture. My experience as a monk taught me that seeking God in community with others made a tremendous impact on my personal spiritual search. In fact, the same cosmic energy that is impelling us to seek for answers to the eternal questions on our own is encouraging us to do it in the company of others. When you and I connect with other people who are on a similar spiritual journey, our experience is immeasurably enhanced and supported, and so is theirs. Group endeavor, we are finding, can itself be a spiritual practice. Forming a group of like-minded people to engage some humanitarian effort, for instance, magnifies the effect of the effort, at the same time amplifying our essential connection to one another. Since we are all facets of the One, anything we undertake together moves everything upward exponentially for everyone.

I have seen firsthand how powerful group endeavor can be, especially when it is put to use in the service of personal transformation. With two colleagues, Beverly Nelson, a holistic psychologist, and Michael Herbert, an intuitive body worker, I conduct guided retreats in San Miguel de Allende, Mexico. We chose this Spanish colonial mountain town not only for its extraordinary beauty but also because it is removed from the cultural grid, unfamiliar and somewhat exotic. Outside their comfort zone, people who come to us are able to concentrate more fully on their inner "unfinished business." Our LifePath retreats are designed for seekers who are on a quest for purpose and meaning and direction in their lives. Participants come from many places around the world to do their personal growth work with others as part of a small group. The group members hold each other's intentions for positive change and mirror each other's transformative process. During the weeklong program, we observe old psychological and emotional wounds heal rapidly and almost spontaneously as group members interact with one another. The effect is something like what happens when ten people move a car that is stuck in the mud. You can try to do it alone, but you will have a tough time of it; if nine more people join in, the car gets back on the road quickly. More than that, a spiritual bond forms among the car pushers. For a few moments, there is a feeling of camaraderie, a shared heart opening, and, like the scientific theory of entanglement, a sense that spiritual nonseparability has been achieved.

If you feel drawn to continue your personal growth work with us, either by yourself or with a small group, you can find out more about LifePath at www.LifePathRetreats.com.

As part of your personal spiritual search, I encourage you to find like-minded people to share your process. In your synergistic encounters, when you offer your direct experience of your spiritual path and receive another's direct experience in return, one and one equal three and vistas open for you onto undreamed of realms—it is a spiritual law.

At the beginning of this book, I told you about the vision that came to me quite unexpectedly a few years ago during that meditation-for-stress-reduction class. I saw myself as a big transparent bubble, and I was merging with another bubble to tell my life's story. While I was communicating this present lifetime, I felt complete and utter fulfillment, as if I had accomplished my life's purpose. In that moment, I knew deep in my heart that all I had to do to be happy was simply live my life with as much awareness as I could muster, so that I could tell my story to another bubble, and then another, learning more spiritual lessons with each retelling. In this way I open myself to the rich and wonderful soul stories of others.

No matter how the future unfolds for us as a species on this garden planet—and for you and me individually—in the next few crucial years, never have we had a better opportunity to fulfill our spiritual longings and bring heaven to earth than at this shining moment. In the past few years, we have put many things in place to begin to accomplish the eons-old aspirations of our ancestors for the fullness of life. Primary among them are communications technologies that are advancing with mind-boggling speed and complexity. Over an unimaginably short time, we have leapt from telegraph to telephone to radio to television to the Internet, communicating with one another as we never have before in all of human history. The next advances surely will be in direct telepathy, allowing us to join our minds and hearts together at will. We are made, it appears, for merging.

I believe we have brought about these communication miracles ultimately to convey high spiritual understanding to each other. In 312 B.C., at the beginning of the age that is coming to a close in our own time, Roman engineers commenced work on the Via Appia. It was the first of what would become a vast network of unprecedented hard-wearing roads leaving Rome and extending first to the seaport of Neapolis (Naples) and then to several cities along the Aegean coast of Italy, becoming the vital link to Greece and the East. The Romans built their roads to move their legions, which is to say for conquest. But roads go in two directions. What left the backwater province of Judea and came back to conquer Rome—and after that, over fifty-three thousand miles of Roman roadway to the farthest reaches of the mighty empire, from Scotland to the borders of Persia— was the spiritual message of unconditional love.

At the dawn of our new epoch, we are being offered another chance, perhaps a final one, to "harness the energies of love," as Teilhard de Chardin says. Maybe the fantastic highways we are building in the air will bring all of us together at last in a planetwide family reunion, to make the age at hand truly a Golden Age. And the message from milestone to milestone along those roads is what we knew in the beginning and forgot: that we came here to love one another, always and everywhere, to love one another.

Afterword

BIBLIOGRAPHY

Alcott, A. B. *How Like an Angel Came I Down: Conversations with Children on the Gospels.* Great Barrington, Mass.: Lindisfarne Books, 1991.

Armstrong, K. *A History of God: The 4,000-Year Quest of Judaism, Christianity and Islam.* New York: Ballantine Books, 1994.

Armstrong, K. *The Battle for God.* New York: Ballantine Books, 2001.

Armstrong, K. *Buddha.* New York: Penguin, 2004.

Campbell, J. *The Hero with a Thousand Faces.* Princeton, N.J.: Princeton University Press, 1949.

Campbell, J. *Transformations of Myth Through Time.* New York: HarperCollins, 1990.

Carmody, D. L., and Carmody, J. *Mysticism: Holiness East and West.* New York: Oxford University Press, 1996.

Carse, J. *Finite and Infinite Games.* New York: Macmillan, 1986.

Chopra, D. *How to Know God: The Soul's Journey into the Mystery of Mysteries.* New York: Three Rivers Press (Random House), 2001.

Dispenza, J. *Live Better Longer.* San Francisco: HarperSanFrancisco, 1997.

Dossey, L. *Healing Words: The Power of Prayer and the Practice of Medicine.* New York: HarperCollins, 1993.

Dyer, W. *The Power of Intention.* Carlsbad, Calif.: Hay House, 2004.

Eichenbaum, D. *Soul Signs: Harness the Power of Your Sun Sign and Become the Person You Were Meant to Be.* New York: Fireside (Simon & Schuster), 1998.

Eisler, R. *The Chalice and the Blade: Our History, Our Future.* San Francisco: HarperSanFrancisco, 1988.

Eliade, M. *Shamanism: Archaic Techniques of Ecstasy.* Princeton, N.J.: Princeton University Press, 1972.

Forman, R.K.C. *Mysticism, Mind, and Consciousness.* Albany: State University of New York Press, 1999.

Fox, M. *The Coming of the Cosmic Christ.* San Francisco: HarperSanFrancisco, 1988.

Gallup Jr., G., and Jones, T. *The Next American Spirituality: Finding God in the Twenty-First Century.* Colorado Springs, Colo.: Chariot Victor, 2000.

Goldsmith, J. S. *The Thunder of Silence.* San Francisco: HarperSanFrancisco, 1993.

Gould, S. J. *Hen's Teeth and Horse's Toes.* New York: Norton, 1984.

Hamilton, E. *Mythology.* New York: Little, Brown, 1942.

Harris, M. E. *Remembering Black Mountain College.* Asheville, N.C.: Black Mountain Press, 1998.

Harris, S. *The End of Faith: Religion, Terror, and the Future of Reason.* New York: Norton, 2004.

Hartmann, T. *The Last Hours of Ancient Sunlight: The Fate of the World and What We Can Do Before It's Too Late.* (Rev. and updated ed.). New York: Three Rivers Press (Random House), 2004.

Hubbard, B. M. *Emergence: The Shift from Ego to Essence.* Charlottesville, Va.: Hampton Roads Publishing Co., 2001.

James, W. *The Varieties of Religious Experience: A Study in Human Nature.* New York: Collier, 1961. (Originally published 1902.)

Jung, C. G. *Modern Man in Search of a Soul.* New York: Harvest/HBJ Book, 1955.

Jung, C. G. *Man and His Symbols.* (Reissue ed.) New York: Laurel (Dell), 1968.

Kapleau, P. *The Three Pillars of Zen: Teaching, Practice, and Enlightenment.* New York: Doubleday Anchor, 1989.

Katie, B. *Loving What Is: Four Questions That Can Change Your Life.* New York: Three Rivers Press (Random House), 2003.

Kavanaugh, K. *John of the Cross: Selected Writings.* Mahwah, N.J.: Paulist Press, 1987.

Kosmin, B. A., Mayer, E., and Keysar, A. *American Religious Identification Survey 2001.* New York: Graduate Center, City University of New York, 2001.

Kübler-Ross, E. *On Death and Dying.* (Reprint ed.) New York: Scribner, 1997.

Kuhn, T. S. *The Structure of Scientific Revolutions.* (3rd ed.) Chicago: University of Chicago Press, 1996.

Lucas, S. *Bloodlines of the Soul: Karmic Patterns in Past Life Dreams.* Lincoln, Nebr.: iUniverse, 2005.

Lukas, M., and Lukas, E. *Teilhard.* Garden City, N.Y.: Doubleday, 1977.

232

MacLaine, S. *Out on a Limb.* New York: Bantam, 1983.

Madigan, S., and Ward, B. (eds.). *Mystics, Visionaries, and Prophets: A Historical Anthology of Women's Spiritual Writings.* Minneapolis: Fortress Press, 1998.

Marcuse, H. *Legacies of Dachau: The Uses and Abuses of a Concentration Camp, 1933–2001.* New York: Cambridge University Press, 2001.

Maslow, A. *Motivation and Personality.* New York: HarperCollins, 1987.

Merton, T. *New Seeds of Contemplation.* New York: New Directions, 1972.

Merton, T. *Thoughts in Solitude.* New York: Farrar, Straus, and Giroux, 1999.

Mitchell, S. *Bhagavad Gita: A New Translation.* New York: Three Rivers Press (Random House), 2002.

Muktananda, Swami. *Play of Consciousness: A Spiritual Autobiography.* South Fallsburg, N.Y.: Siddha Yoga Publications, 2000.

Niehardt, J. C. (ed.). *Black Elk Speaks: Being the Life Story of a Holy Man of the Oglala Sioux.* Lincoln: University of Nebraska Press, 1988.

Pearson, C. *Awakening the Heroes Within: Twelve Archetypes to Help Us Find Ourselves and Transform Our World.* San Francisco: HarperSanFrancisco, 1991.

Sagan, C. *The Dragons of Eden: Speculations on the Evolution of Human Intelligence.* New York: Random House, 1977.

Schimmel, A. *Mystical Dimensions of Islam.* Chapel Hill: University of North Carolina Press, 1975.

Sieden, L. S. *Buckminster Fuller's Universe: His Life and Work.* New York: Perseus Books Group, 2000.

Suzuki, D. T. *An Introduction to Zen Buddhism.* New York: Grove Press, 1991.

Teasdale, W. *A Monk in the World: Cultivating a Spiritual Life.* Novato, Calif.: New World Library, 2002.

Teilhard de Chardin, P. *The Phenomenon of Man.* New York: HarperCollins, 1961.

Teilhard de Chardin, P. *The Divine Milieu: An Essay on the Interior Life.* New York: HarperCollins, 1968.

Thomas Aquinas, Saint. *Aquinas's Shorter Summa: Saint Thomas's Own Concise Version of His Summa Theologica.* Manchester, N.H.: Sophia Institute Press, 2001.

Thompson, W. I. *The Time Falling Bodies Take to Light: Mythology, Sexuality and the Origins of Culture.* New York: Palgrave Macmillan, 1996.

Trevelyan, Sir G. "Foreword." In *The Findhorn Garden: Pioneering a New Vision of Humanity and Nature in Cooperation.* Findhorn, Scotland, UK: Findhorn Press, 2003.

United States Catholic Church. *Catechism of the Catholic Church.* (2nd ed.) New York: Doubleday, 2003.

Waters, F. *Mexico Mystique: The Coming Sixth World of Consciousness.* Thousand Oaks, Calif.: Sage, 1975.

Weil, S. *Gravity and Grace.* New York: Putnam, 1952.

Westfall, R. S. *The Trial of Galileo: Bellarmino, Galileo, and the Clash of Two Worlds.* Valparaiso, Ind.: Valparaiso University Press, 1988.

THE AUTHOR

JOSEPH DISPENZA is the award-winning author of *The Way of the Traveler* and *Live Better Longer,* along with other books and articles about living a higher-quality life. He is a former university professor who lived for several years in a monastery learning personal spirituality firsthand. He is the cofounder of LifePath Retreats in San Miguel de Allende, Mexico, where he writes and is in practice as a spiritual counselor.

Dispenza brings to his writing and counseling more than thirty years of teaching and spiritual practice. He entered the Roman Catholic Congregation of Holy Cross early in life and lived as a monk for eight years. Later, he left the monastery to pursue a more active life, working for social change with a number of humanitarian organizations.

After earning a B.A. in the humanities and an M.A. in communication, he was for several years the director of education programs for the American Film Institute in Washington, D.C., and later a story editor for United Artists in Los Angeles. He left Hollywood for Santa Fe, where he took up the life of a writer. *The House of Alarcon,* an epic novel of a Spanish colonial family in New Mexico, was published in the United States and simultaneously in the United Kingdom.

He created a highly successful academic program in Moving Image Arts at the College of Santa Fe and served as its founding chair for six years, while also teaching courses in cinema history and media ethics. After he left academia, he became the director of Parcells Center, an organization established to disseminate information on holistic approaches to wellness.

Dispenza's dream for many years has been to create a retreat program away from the dominant culture for people sincerely seeking to question the great truths of life—to offer to others the unique experiences he had as a monk and a student of spirituality. LifePath, which he cofounded in 2000, is fulfilling that dream.

He is a frequent contributor to several online publications, including Beliefnet.com, Spirituality.com, and Newtopia.com. His articles have appeared in dozens of national magazines, among them *Spirituality and Health, American Way, Massage Magazine, Magical Blend,* and *Yoga Journal.*

{ .. .. }

You can interact online with Joseph Dispenza and other readers of this book. Share your experiences as you walk your own spiritual path: www.josephdispenza.com.

INDEX

Index

Sacred skepticism: aspects of, 41–58; defined, 47. *See also* Doubt
Sacrificial archetype, 45
Sagan, C., 53, 192, 193
Saint Peter's Basilica, 8, 73
Saint-Exupéry, A., 153
Salk, J., 200
San Miguel de Allende, Mexico, 224
Sankara, 203
Santa Fe, New Mexico, experience in, 67–68
Santiago de Compostela, 54
Schedule, importance of a, in monastic life, 153–154
Schizophrenia, 166
Scholasticate, the, 35, 36
Schopenhauer, A., 160
Schweitzer, A., 169, 202, 203, 204
Science: conflict between religion and, 215; discoveries made by, 191–192, 210–211, 219
Science and Health with Key to the Scriptures (Eddy), 197
Scotland, 227
Second Council of Constantinople, 102
Seder, 90
Seeds of Contemplation (Merton), xi
Seeing: giving full attention to, 144; without judging, 69, 128
Seeker archetype, xv, 44, 46, 56, 63, 65. *See also* Spiritual seekers
Self-actualization, 175
Self-awareness, increased, 168
Self-destructive philosophy, 213–214
Self-involvement, 206
Self-love, 137
Self-regulation, 159
Separation, issue of, 139, 192, 194, 200, 213, 222
September 11, 2001, attacks, 216
Service, aspects of, 191–206
Seth Speaks (Roberts), 99
Seventh heaven, the, 185–186

Sex, issue of, 135–139. *See also* Chastity, vow of
Shadow Seekers, 56–58
Shakespeare, W., 208
Shamans, role of, 178, 180, 183
Shame, experiencing, 33, 34
Siddhartha Gautama, 58. *See also* Buddha
Silence, 12, 13, 153, 184
Simplicity, idea of, 126
Sin, 29, 33, 52, 74, 137, 141, 199, 213, 219
Sinister trinity of emotions, letting go of the, 130–131
Situational archetype, 45
Skepticism, defined, 47. *See also* Sacred skepticism
Sky-God religions, 158, 219, 221
Smith, J. H., 187–188
Sobriety, 187, 188
Socrates, 144, 160
Sophists, 160
Soul: definitions of, 102; global, 206; past, as an obstacle, 102–107; taking back your, xi–xix
Soul Signs (Eichenbaum), 217
Soul-mending process, story of a, 107–113
Soviet Union, 216
Species arrogance, results of, 213
Spider-Woman, 222
Spielberg, S., 204
Spiritual attachment, 131–133
Spiritual bond, 225
Spiritual bypass, 97–98, 107, 112
Spiritual identity, essential, recognition of, 185
Spiritual innocence, 152
Spiritual limbo, 35
Spiritual malpractice, 222
Spiritual practice, group endeavor as, 224–224
Spiritual searching/seeking: authentic, by definition, 52; connecting

248

with others during the process of, 224–225; starting in religion, 17–18, 20; willingness to experiment with, 6–7. *See also specific aspects of seeking*

Spiritual seekers: becoming, reason for, xv–xvi, xix; born as, 5; called to be, 43, 44; challenges for, xviii, 58; compulsive, 56–58; defining, xv; fear about, 108; finding a new path as, beginning of, 25; other names for, 46; on a sacred quest, 48; sincere, what comes to, 38; viewpoint requisite for, 52. *See also* Seeker archetype

Spiritual truth, 19, 24, 52, 58, 78, 195

Spiritual void, prospect of a, experiencing, 34

Spiritual weariness, 31

Spirituality: age of, beginning the, 223; authentic, pursuing, 35, 78; evolving sense of, 24; healthy, proof of, xviii; primary principle of, 20; realm of, first experience with, story of, 9–10; versus religion, xvii–xviii; solid, finding, issue of, xiii, xiv; unquestioned or lack of, holding on to, 131–133. *See also specific practices and beliefs*

Spontaneous healings, 201

Sri Sathya Sai Baba, 99

Stonehenge, 54

Storytellers, existing as, 4, 5, 225–226

Structure of Scientific Revolution, The (Kuhn), 18

Subduing the earth, consequences of, 212–213

Success, 204

Summa Theologica (Thomas Aquinas), 22

Sutras of Buddhism, 49

Syncletica, A., 117

T

Tallil Airbase, Iraq, 212

Taoism, 169

Tarot, the, 55

Teasdale, W., 119

Teilhard de Chardin, P., xiv, 36–37, 55, 127, 187, 198, 199, 217, 223, 227

Telepathy, 226

Televangelists, 219–220

Temple School, 151

Ten Commandments, the, 75, 158–159

Tepoztlan, Mexico, 177

Teresa, Mother, 121, 169, 203

Teresa of Avila, Saint, 108, 139, 172

Terrorists, Muslim, 220

Tesla, N., 219

Thanksgiving, prayer of, 94

Theological theories, issue of, 132–133

Theology of escape, 219

Therapy, experimenting with, 55, 99–101

Thomas Aquinas, Saint, 22, 160

Thomas, the Apostle, 30

Thompson, W. I., 220

Thoreau, H. D., 150, 173

Thought-stopping techniques, 149–150

Thunder of Silence, The (Goldsmith), 196–197

Time Falling Bodies Take to Light, The (Thompson), 220

Torah, the, 48

Toxic feelings: exaggeration stemming from, 148; letting go of, 130–131; taking responsibility for, 168

Traherne, T., 152